W9-BRH-221

HABITS of a Priestly HEART

FR. EUGENE HEMRICK

Habits of a Priestly Heart
Fr. Eugene Hemrick

Associate Publisher and Editor: Jerry Galipeau
Production Editor: Mary Brewick
Copy Editor: Marcia T. Lucey
Cover Design: Chris Broquet
Typesetter and Book Design: Denise C. Durand
Director of Publications: Mary Beth Kunde-Anderson
Production Manager: Deb Johnston
Rights and Permissions Manager: Michele vonEbers

WLP 001760
ISBN 978-1-58459-442-0

WLP Customer Care: 1 800 566-6150
Toll-free fax: 1 888 957-3291
wlpcs@jspaluch.com
www.wlpmusic.com

To Mickey Paluch and
Bill and Mary Lou Paluch Rafferty,
for their undying dedication to promoting
and supporting vocations to the religious life.

CONTENTS

FOREWORD

Father Eugene Hemrick's extensive research, writings, and his Web site, The National Institute for the Renewal of the Priesthood[1], reflect a man who has a deep, loving interest in priests and the priesthood of Christ. His writings include such topics as "Keeping Priests Healthy," "What Priests Want From Retirement," "Coping with a Church and Priesthood That Seem to Be Coming Apart," "Priests Can Be Youthful at Any Age," "A Beleaguered Priesthood in Need of Spirit," and "A Priesthood Re-energized." He has also addressed the questions What underlies the priesthood shortage? What's behind the crisis in the priesthood? Father, how do you see your priesthood?

Father Hemrick's book is designed to help today's priests better understand, accept, and live with new—and sometimes overwhelming—challenges of the third millennium.

Today's priests face heretofore unimagined challenges that are not only new to this country, but to the history of the priesthood. Some fifty years ago there were enough priests available so that even the smallest of small rural parishes were staffed by a resident priest. In many dioceses it was common to remain an assistant pastor for twenty years or more because all the pastorates were filled. Now it is not unusual to be appointed pastor within a few years after ordination.

The shortage of priests has created two major changes in our times: the advent of mega-parishes and pastors serving more than one parish. Parishes with as many as three thousand-plus families function under a pastor who does not have an associate or assistant, needs and receives help from retired or religious priests, and is assisted by professional lay staff and volunteers in all other areas. Pastors in such parishes normally spend most of their time managing staff and less time responding to pastoral problems.

The priest who serves as pastor for more than one parish is forever commuting to and from parishes and communicating via cell phone, faxes, and e-mails with his support teams. If he has three, four, or more parishes, he will spend a large portion of each day in a car. In many cases, celebrating Mass at every parish on a weekend is too demanding and nearly impossible. Hence he finds himself commissioning deacons or laypersons to lead Communion services in place of a Mass. Priests in these and similar situations face extraordinary challenges—so extraordinary and overwhelming that they could lose perspective of who they are as priests and what being Church really means.

This book is designed to help priests more fully understand, accept, and live with these new millennium challenges. Father Hemrick identifies the problems and recalls many of his experiences with wholesome priests who give evidence of a priestly heart that is alive and well, priestly hearts centered in Christ. His examples of priests he has known and studied offer us insight into habits that have brought them to a healthy and joy-filled life. Every priest can find something in this work that is helpful, affirming, and confirming. This book is also for non-ordained persons seeking enriching habits that will lift them to a higher level of holiness and wholesomeness.

Abbot Dismas Kalcic, osB
St. Procopius Abbey, Lisle, Ilinois

ACKNOWLEDGMENTS

My deepest gratitude goes to the following for making this work possible: my brother Joe and his wife, Dotty; my sister Ann Marie and her husband, David; my sister Mary Ellen, her husband, Doug; and her son and daughter-in-law, Jonathan and Rachel Puskas. Thanks to the support and encouragement of my nephew Chris Hemrick and his wife, Marcy, I trained for a ten-mile run that kept me physically fit during the trying moments of writing this book.

Special thanks go to those who, in one way or other, are the inspiration behind this book: Bishops Joseph Imesch, Peter Sartain, Daniel Kucera, OSB, and William Friend; Roger Kaffer, Ray Goedert, and Tim Lyne; Fathers Raymond Garbin, Rollins Lambert, Dan Coughlin, Dan Mayall, Mike O'Keefe, Joe McCloskey, SJ, John Crossin, OSFS, Bob Pelton, CSC, and Jim Murphy; Monsignors Neil Mahoney, Richard Burton, Mike Wilson, and Charles Antonicelli; and dear friends Frank Cunningham, David Gibson, Regina Grunert, Richard McCord, Gary and Robyn Bockweg, Joe Jones, Elsa Thompson, Vincent and Jane Coats, Glen and Kay Elsasser, Ron Hindle, Ralph and Mary Dwan, Ray and Jean Hartman, Bob Krieg, and Tim and Jean Unsworth.

I would be remiss if I didn't mention Doctors James Youniss, Dean Hoge, William D'Antonio, Steven Schneck, and Robert O'Gorman. Special thanks to the people of St. Vincent's Archabbey in Latrobe, Pennsylvania; St. Procopius Abbey in Lisle, Illinois; the Catholic Church Extension Society; the J.S. Paluch Company; The Life Cycle Institute at The Catholic University of America; The Center for Applied Research in the Apostolate at Georgetown University; and the parishioners of St. Joseph on Capitol Hill in Washington, D.C.; St. Petronille in Glen Ellyn, Illinois; and St. Raphael in Rockville, Maryland.

Thanks especially must be extended to the faculty and administrative members of the Washington Theological Union, where this book was written.

INTRODUCTION

"WHAT ARE THE HABITS of the heart that move us, the beliefs and practices that shape our character and form our social order? . . . How ought we to live? How do we think about how to live? Who are we as Americans? What is our character?"[2]

In 1985, sociologist Robert Bellah and his associates raised these questions in their highly acclaimed book *Habits of the Heart*, which provided an in-depth look into the heart of America dating from the Founding Fathers to present times. *Habits of a Priestly Heart*, like Bellah's book, explores practices, beliefs, and habits. Rather than studying the heart of America, it explores our priestly heart and what most defines and shapes our character.

This book is the result of thirty years of conducting research on Roman Catholic priests and sharing ideals and concerns with them at retreats, convocations, and clergy days. It is also the fruit of experiencing the priesthood during several bicycling jaunts across this country and Europe. Thanks to these adventures, I was blessed with extraordinary glimpses into our priestly heart.

One of those impressive glimpses occurred early in my priesthood while cycling from Wall, South Dakota, to Seattle, Washington. During that venture, my cycling partner—who was a college student—and I spent a day with Jesuit missionaries serving American Indians in Rapid City, South Dakota. When we finished our trip, I asked my cycling partner what most impressed him. He replied, "Those Jesuits: they were real men focused on serving the American Indian."

We encountered this dedication repeatedly as we moved from one Indian reservation to the next while cycling through Montana and the state of Washington. As beautiful as was the countryside, the reservations were bleak. White crosses dotted our routes, indicating places where automobile deaths had claimed the lives of American Indians. Many of the accidents, we learned, were the result of driving while intoxicated. As impoverished as were the Indian reservations, and as difficult as it was to minister to those afflicted with alcoholism, the missionary zeal of the priests was awesome. Complaints were few as they served a culture that had, in many cases, been decimated by unscrupulous settlers and government officials.

While cycling through southern Germany, in my discussions with priests in Karlsruhe I experienced another heartening dimension of our priesthood. The priests I met were startling examples of what it means to be "dead serious." Although our conversation flitted back and forth in various languages, we were all basically singing in the same choir. What especially touched me was their burning desire to confront the proliferation of nuclear arms head-on, and to champion the philosophy characterized by the phrase "small is beautiful." They were cutting-edge priests far ahead of their times, defending the conservation of our resources and trying to prevent a nuclear Armageddon. Applying the word of God to post-modern justice issues was at the core of their priestly heart.

In more recent years, I've spent considerable time giving clergy days. One clergy day I will never forget was for the priests of the Diocese of Brooklyn, New York, who were planning the future of the priesthood in their diocese. At first our discussions revolved around the issues of clustering priests, avoiding burnout, multiculturalism, lack of finances, and the challenge of too much paperwork required by "downtown." At one point in the discussions, one priest suddenly stood up and said, "These discussions are all well and good, but what are we really about? Isn't it Christ and making him better known?" Within seconds the entire discussion switched from speaking about problems to discussing better ways of evangelizing those among themselves. The conversation became Christ-centered, reflecting the true soul of a priestly heart.

During a visit to Rome, I had a conversation with an Italian cardinal that raised an appreciation of our American priesthood I already possessed, but had not yet vocalized as vociferously as I was about to in this particular conversation. To avoid using my poor Italian, I asked for an interpreter, since the cardinal didn't speak English. The cardinal asked me, "Father, how do you explain this: African priests are not so good as organizers like you Americans, ah, but they are so very spiritual. American priests are very good organizers, ah, but they aren't so spiritual?"

I started to reply in English for the interpreter, but suddenly I remembered many of the conversations I had shared with priests while on retreats with them. I realized the cardinal was dead wrong! I was so struck by this realization and wanted him to know this that I went into Italian and said, "With all due respect, I know the heart of our American priests, and if there is one true way to describe them, it is their desire to be holy!"

And then there was a cardinal, who was a priest first and foremost, and who was all heart. At one point during my lengthy tenure with the U.S. bishops' conference, I began to have doubts about remaining in my position there. As happens in all institutions, new people had been hired, changes had occurred, and my life at the conference just wasn't what it had once been. I realized that I could either hang in there, remaining at the conference, or, as we say in Washington, D.C., remember that "there is life beyond the Beltway" and seek out that life. Cardinal Joseph Bernardin had brought me to the bishops' conference, and over time we became very good friends. In my quandary, I decided to call him for advice. A sister answered the phone and gently said, "Father, the cardinal is very sick. Please call him later." I told her to forget my call, but apparently she didn't and passed it on to the cardinal. Within an hour my phone rang and I was greeted with, "Happy Valentine's Day, Gene; what can I do for you?" What I hadn't known when I made the call was that Cardinal Bernardin was in extreme pain because chemotherapy was weakening his bones, causing them to fracture. Despite his pain, he was still a shepherd, and thought of others first. His priestly heart continued to guide him in his suffering.

These experiences are but a few of the inspiring examples of a priestly heart. It is a heart in which

- There is devotion to helping the poorest of poor.

- There is a deep concern about our world's future.

- Christ is the center of its existence.

- Personal suffering doesn't get in the way of helping others.

As inspiring as is our priestly heart, some priests have not stayed true to it, and others have lost a desire to be a priest. In many ways, this has been disheartening to those of us who enjoyed their camaraderie and friendship.

Several years ago, in my capacity as director of research for the bishops' conference, I commissioned a study on the number of priests the United States would have by the year 2005. To obtain the numbers needed to complete this study, I visited dioceses across the nation and accessed their archives. I will never forget going into Chicago's archdiocesan archives and the sorrow I felt when I learned just how many great priests and classmates with whom I was in the seminary had left the priesthood. No doubt some of them had good reasons for leaving, but for me, as for others, this took some of the heart out of our priesthood because many of them had reflected the very heart of the priesthood at its best.

Another disheartening experience occurred when I arrived home one afternoon only to see the pastor I was living with packing. He had been told to leave the parish immediately because of sexual abuse allegations. This was a very dark moment, but even darker was the experience of having several close priest friends defrocked because of accusations.

I believe that those of us who know brother priests who have lost touch with their priestly hearts have it within ourselves to pray that their priestly hearts be restored. The Canticle of Ezekiel captures our desire for their welfare: "A new heart I will give you, and a new spirit I will put within you; and I will remove from your body the heart of stone and give you a heart of flesh" (Ezekiel 36:26).

These not uncommon examples of priests who leave on their own or who have been dismissed teach us how easy it is for our priestly heart to be wounded, hardened, and disheartened. How we can restore the wounded heart and refresh the healthy heart is the ultimate purpose of this book.

Three decades of studying the priesthood and four decades as a priest have led me to believe six priestly habits are absolutely indispensable for a wholesome priestly heart.

1. Resisting the temptation to think that once we are ordained we are defined

2. Growing in kindness and holding at bay anything that threatens it

3. Keeping our contemplative edge sharp

4. Embracing ongoing education as an essential part of our ministry

5. Including physical fitness as a part of our lives which refreshes us to minister in the best way we can

6. Creating a new synergism of international priests, deacons, the laity, and us

When we reflect on these six habits, we cannot but notice that they start with priestly identity, spirituality, education, and fitness, and only then address collaboration with others. Here we need to ask, "Doesn't this smack of clericalism and navel gazing? Aren't we about service to others first, and only then about serving ourselves?"

Borrowing from an age-old athletic principle reveals our answer: we must first get ourselves in condition before attempting to cope well with the challenging conditions of our people and Church. In the world of sports, diets are carefully chosen, unique exercises are crafted, and attitudes are formulated to produce the best frame of mind for winning. Sound self-conditioning must precede the rigors of the contest. This principle echoes the wisdom of the great ancient philosophers who counsel us, "Know thyself first!" and Christ our Lord who taught, "Physician, heal yourself first."

Like most priests today, I have celebrated three or four Masses, buried someone, and counseled others all in the same day. At the end of a day like this, it is common to feel worn out and to wonder what more needs to be done to invigorate our priesthood. *Habits of a Priestly Heart* is a compilation of habits aimed at arming us with the means for generating a wholesome and joyous priesthood that is fit to respond to the new challenges of the third millennium.

If you don't know where you are going, you will probably end up somewhere else.[3]

LAURENCE J. PETER (1919–1990), CANADIAN WRITER

1

KEEPING OUR PURPOSE UPDATED

HOW IMPORTANT IS it that we meditate on the purpose of our priesthood? Does it really matter whether we attempt to develop greater clarity about the purpose of our lives? Yes, it is essential not only for priests, but for everyone! Why be so emphatic? Two reasons in particular stand out: clarity of purpose is the basis of zeal, and more importantly, it is our best means for keeping our vocation alive. The more we work at it, the better the chance of remaining a happy, fulfilled priest.

During a particularly beautiful summer evening in Washington, D.C., I ambled down to our city's annual folk festival on the mall. Once there, I experienced an unexpected lesson in zeal. In front of a bandstand, young people were merrily dancing in a big circle. As I watched, a young man from the group approached me and asked, "Would you mind if I talked with you?" He told me his group was one of the new millennium tribes of Israel founded on the principle of living together in peace. "The reason we dance in circles," he pointed out, "is that a circle denotes unity." He then declared that today's corrupt society needs his community more than ever. I let him go on for a few minutes, and then leveled with him, saying, "I am a Catholic priest, a priest of four decades."

He congratulated me and then commented, "Then you know what I am talking about," and continued proselytizing. He argued that the Catholic Church had gone wrong, and the book of Revelation says God transfers his graces to other religions when this happens. We talked religion for over an hour, and I must admit he listened as intently to me as I did to him. "I deeply admire your zeal," I told him. "It is this same first zeal I had when entering the priesthood. Please don't lose it." He in turn said, "Before you read the literature I gave you, I ask you this favor: pray that God makes your mind as open as that of a child." During the time we were together that young man never stopped trying to convert me, even though he knew who I was.

The meaning of "zeal" comes from another root word meaning "fire." That young man started gently with me, but once he got going, he was like fire that feeds on dry underbrush. Every argument I raised fueled his counterarguments. Even though many wouldn't agree with his ideals, his zeal simply could not be faulted. He had a clear purpose. Knowing what he was striving for was the basis for his enthusiasm. Just as a well-defined purpose drove this young man's zeal, so too does it drive us.

In 1995, the National Catholic Educational Association, my colleagues, and I conducted a study on the most effective priests in our country. The study became the basis of the book *Grace Under Pressure*. In our interviews, one thing stood out most: those priests found to be most effective were filled with zeal. One major reason for this was that they did not take for granted being once and forever clearly defined as a priest. Let's listen to their meditations on their purpose and note the zest this generates.

Dick, 62, a Southern pastor, reflects on his life as a "change agent." He said,

> I am never satisfied that I have conquered all the hills that God has put in front of me. I am always looking for a new one to climb. And that has been tremendously life-giving throughout my life. I think the bottom line is being a change agent. That to me is what has given me the biggest challenge and made the juices flow. When I look at something, I see it in the words of Robert Kennedy—I look at things and people and say, why? And then I say, Why not, why not? That invigorates me to say let's push that horizon a little bit further and look beyond the wall.[4]

A priest named Andrew takes inspiration from his namesake.

> One of the things that gives me life, I would say, is recognition of limits. Using my own namesake in the gospel, Andrew might be in some sense an explanation. He doesn't turn up too often. But two of the times he turns up, all he does is introduce somebody else. That is it. He didn't take on the responsibility of converting them. He left that to Christ, but he introduced Peter and he introduced the young fellow with the loaves and fishes. And in some sense I think if I recognize this, I realize I am not called to do everything. That in some sense I'm just called to introduce and we leave it up to God and up to the grace of God after that.[5]

Don, 48, a pastor from the Midwest, describes priests as "walking symbols." He said,

> What goes on with us is way beyond our personalities and our talents. We are walking symbols in some ways. And it's a lot bigger than I am and what I've learned. I don't know how to balance it. I spent a lot of years in my priesthood trying to be one of the people–'I am a plain old person like all the rest of you. I struggle like all the rest of you.' And there was something holy, I think, in that. But there is another side of that truth and there is almost a shaman kind of dimension to what we do. We are walking symbols.[6]

Yet another priest told us,

> For me the most life-giving reality is the Paschal Mystery. The community I belong to stresses very strongly the Paschal Mystery and the reality of passing over, that we pass over from who we are and what we are and empty out into other people's lives and other people's cultures.[7]

In his book *Priests Among Men*, Cardinal Emmanuel Suhard gives us yet another dimension of a priest seeking clarity of purpose. In it, we see an earnest pastor examining his role in a parish that is a mix of conservatives and liberals. Suhard pictures him "patiently comparing point by point his two guiding plans. The old plan of the church in the Christian community has its islands of influence, its strongholds and its areas of habitual Christian practice. The other plan, of the new city, has its quick bridgeheads, its centers of spontaneous interest and its unexpected religious movements."[8] Suhard continues, "He will know no rest until the two plans run together, until they coincide to form the one 'city' in truth and love."[9]

In the picture Suhard paints, we encounter a pastor endeavoring to fulfill the responsibility of bridge builder, unifier, and reconciler. He's not only studying his parish, but he is working at clarifying his purpose: making both plans of his parish "coincide to form the one 'city' in truth and love." Note how his purpose feeds his zeal: "He will know no rest until the two plans run together."

Two recent instances in my own priesthood provide further examples of how much our priesthood brims with purposefulness—a purposefulness just waiting to be clarified so that it can increase our zeal.

It's my morning custom to listen to classical music while driving to work. On one such morning, Dennis Owens, who hosts an FM radio station in Washington, D.C., announced he was retiring. After years of getting used to his voice, I suddenly realized it would no longer greet me. It was as if I had lost a dear friend. Suddenly it hit me. As priests, we are also like him. We are a familiar voice to our people. Sometimes it's a voice with the "fire in the belly" that the renowned homilist Father Walter Burkhardt said should fill our homilies. At other times, it's compassionate or serious. It then occurred to me, "We are more than a voice! The words we speak contain a spirit, not just any spirit, but a unique priestly spirit! Each time we celebrate Mass, give a homily, or converse with our people, we are that spirit."

Some time after this realization, I had an unexpected conversation with a stranger that led to an even more profound realization of this spirit and its purpose in life. A few days after the devastating tsunami of 2004, I met this stranger accidentally while crossing the street. When he learned I was a priest, he told me he wasn't Catholic, but then he began confessing to me as if he were one. I thought to myself, "He doesn't know me, so why open up to me?" Upon further reflection, I came to realize that this man was distraught by the meaningless destruction of the tsunami. He was searching for a purpose. Here was a priest he felt might give him more clarity on the matter.

No doubt each of us has had this experience. And no doubt it has caused us to realize that unlike other callings, ours forms us as unique representatives of Christ the Lord to whom people turn to better understand God's ways. How many times have we experienced people asking us, "Father, please pray for me"? But why do people need our prayers? Why not pray directly to God? Isn't it because we are somehow expected to be a special link between God and humankind?

While watching a scene from the movie *The Godfather Part III*, I had another one of those "Aha-now-I-see-it" experiences that add even greater clarity to our purpose. Against the backdrop of a monastery courtyard, mafia boss Michael Corleone meets with Cardinal Lamberto of the Vatican to discuss the affairs of the Ambrosian Bank. During their conversation, Michael has a diabetic attack. Lamberto immediately calls to his aide, asking him to fetch orange juice and sweets. In a fit of panic, Michael gulps them down. When he finally stabilizes, Lamberto looks into his soul and sees that something more than diabetes is ailing Michael. Then quietly and in an inviting tone he asks Michael if he would like to confess. This Michael does. Later Michael tells his sister Connie of the incident. Upon hearing this, she becomes outraged and cries out, asking Michael how he could have told all the family secrets to this man. Michael replies, "It was the man, a real priest."

We see in the character of Lamberto a priest first and a cardinal second, a priest who intuits in Michael a conscience in conflict with itself. Instead of probing, scolding, and questioning, Lamberto is simply an inviting presence. He discerns Michael's pain, looks into his soul, and then allows himself to become a conduit for God's grace. He is a man who has cultivated a profound sense of what it means to be a priest, a real priest, the personification of Christ amongst us.

Whenever we speak of being a real person, we are also talking about authenticity. The word "authentic" means "to be oneself." In the character of Cardinal Lamberto, we see a man who has a clear picture of his true self as a priest. He reflects a priestly principle well worth treasuring: the more we clarify and develop our purpose, the more we become our true selves and the way God intended us to be. Purpose, authenticity, and being a real priest are complementary.

I have been blessed to have met several "Cardinal Lambertos", priests who knew how to be present to others without invading their space or privacy. When they spoke, you heard the real person: no acting, no self-promotion, just a selfless, humble person who reflected authenticity par excellence! Looking into their eyes, you sensed a person who was solid. When you looked into their soul, you saw Christ. Having now reflected on the depths to which purpose can take us, we need to ask what might be a good habit to cultivate for growing in it.

In the late '60s and early '70s, Doctor Viktor Frankl's logotherapy and the principle of will-to-meaning were highly acclaimed by the world of religion. When applied to our priesthood, will-to-meaning teaches us that the more we seek new and deeper purposes in our ministry, the greater the probability of it growing in wholesomeness. The less this happens, the greater the possibility of losing our meaning, and, God forbid, our vocation.

During World War II, Frankl was imprisoned for three years in Auschwitz, Dachau, and several other concentration camps. In the camps, he used his psychiatric background to study the reasons why some prisoners lived and others died. Some were dying who should have survived, whereas others lived who should have died. The difference, he learned, was will-to-meaning. This discovery led to the basis of his logotherapy.

Frankl learned that survivors who put meaning into their meaningless situations were able to withstand pain, poor health, and the crushing fear of death. Those who died lost desire and stopped seeing meaning in anything. In doing so, they confirmed the principle that without purpose, there is little to live for. The antithesis of this teaches us that clarifying purpose is our best means for generating life-giving hope in our ministry. In my lifetime I have known people who suffered severe depression. They often confide that losing meaning in life and the thoughts of suicide this loss generates are depression's greatest scourge.

When the practices of will-to-meaning and cultivating purposefulness are absent, a crucial source of our vitality is lost. We might not die physically, but we could very well end up being among the walking dead. I believe that neglecting the continued renewal of our purposefulness is a major reason many priests have left active ministry and why others who still may be on the books have lost their drive.

In the 2007 study *Experiences of Priests Ordained Five to Nine Years*, one priest surveyed reflected on one of several reasons priests resign: "There were twelve of us ordained that year. We lost one man a year for the first six years . . . Some of them just couldn't deal with the expectations that were heaped on them when they got to a parish."[10]

When we summarize all the reasons that may have caused priests to leave active ministry, lack of meaningful purpose is at their core. Let's take a look at some of those reasons and see how true this is.

The growing phenomenon of the priest as "lone ranger" has put the priesthood in peril. As we increasingly become lone rangers, we risk losing priests because of this new "lone" phenomenon. At the moment—and probably for the rest of our lives—we will be living in an age of bilocation-ministry-sacramental-excessiveness because we are called to serve multiple parishes.

On the sacramental level, we are experiencing the violation of the wise maxim "All things in moderation." Too many sacraments administered too often in too short a time reduce us to robots. It is becoming more difficult to model Christ, who frequently withdrew from the crowds to make the time and space needed to be with his Father.

In my first assignment as a priest, I experienced an unforgettable example of sacramental excessiveness that taught me how detrimental it is to our ministry. At the time, I lived with four priests who came up with the idea of each of us taking a Sunday in which we preached at all the Masses. After listening to ourselves five times in a row on our appointed Sunday, the practice immediately stopped: staying fresh and energetic was impossible! We literally ran ourselves—and our homilies—into the ground.

Lack of imagination is another reason priests leave. Some never ventured to imagine themselves in the many roles they fulfill; for example, seeing themselves as walking symbols, change agents, or doctors of souls possessing a unique priestly spirit. By not stretching their imaginations, two things happen: 1) they deprive themselves of an excellent means for expanding their purpose, and 2) they do not learn any new and exciting dimensions of who they are as a priest.

On this last point—expanding our imagination—I never thought when I was ordained that we would experience the exodus of outstanding priests that occurred. We lived in an age that was coined "this confident Church." We seemingly knew our purpose, were very well respected, and were defined by our surroundings. This created a confident priesthood. Suddenly, in the '60s and '70s, everything changed, as thousands of priests no longer were sure of their purpose. In this confusion—and mainly because they had not re-imagined themselves—some priests resigned because their original purpose and commitment gave way to other purposes. It may have been a woman's love, a desire for peace they couldn't find in a dramatically changed ministry, or the realization that they knew that they simply weren't being priests.

Feelings of having been sold out also played a substantial role in the exodus of priests. A number of dyed-in-the-wool pre-Vatican II priests felt betrayed by the so-called radical changes of the council. When they voiced their disappointments over the changes, you could almost hear Psalm 55 in the background.

> It is not enemies who taunt me—
> > I could bear that;
> it is not adversaries who deal insolently
> > with me—
> > I could hide from them.
> But it is you, my equal,
> > my companion, my familiar friend.
> > > (Psalm 55:12–13)

The renowned moral theologian Father Bernard Haring gives us another dimension of the exodus when he states that an unrealistic understanding of church, our secular world, and the ever-present struggle between an ecclesial priesthood and the one priesthood we receive in baptism also contributed to priests leaving. He writes,

> We see before us a great company of zealous priests who are wearing themselves out—physically, psychically, spiritually—in continuous activity for their flock. Their activities increase under pressure from a society in which quantitative achievement is especially honored. There are,

too, a great many unsatisfied, even frustrated, priests whose example discourage priestly vocations.

Many are wounded so deeply because they do not grasp the true identity of their vocation and are unable to discern the signs of the times. Some have received a lopsided formation, marked by legalism in moral theology, formalism in liturgy, and a static view of Church. How can they feel at home in a Church which understands itself as a pilgrim Church? There are also priests who gladly accept the Vatican II interpretation of Church, but are unable to find an interpretation of ministerial priesthood corresponding to it. In their confusion, many find it difficult to accept the co-responsibility and cooperation of lay people.[11]

In these observations, Haring points to three ongoing challenges that have the power to knock out our purposefulness. The first challenge involves ministering to a culture inundated with secularism, materialism, relativism, and self-centeredness. Not only does this environment tempt us to join it, it also goes contrary to our mission of proclaiming the God who desires humility, self-sacrifice, and poverty of spirit. Taking on this culture and fighting its temptations often makes us weary. Weariness has an ominous way of depleting our zeal. Worse than this, it often leads us to second-guess our own worth and weakens our commitment.

The second challenge we face is the need to evaluate our vision of church and ask, do we see it as a pilgrim church? Much of the time, ours is a very agreeable faith community and a delight to serve. But it can also be like the hard-hearted Hebrews who were forever testing the faith of Moses. In my first assignment, I lived with a priest who taught me how true this is. One day, while I was waxing eloquent about our role as shepherds, he abruptly interrupted and asked, "Gino, have you ever tended sheep?" "No," I replied, but then tried to justify myself. "My grandfather was a shepherd in Italy and I did learn something about shepherding from him." He then said bluntly, "Gino, sheep stink! Don't forget that!" How right he was! All we need to do is change the furniture in church, open the church late, or make parishioners uncomfortable in our homilies to experience the stink this creates.

The third challenge to our purposefulness is to ask, are we *the* teacher, as some priests have indicated in our studies? Or are we *a* teacher among colleagues learning from each other? If we see our purpose as the one and only teacher, this is problematic because it tends to diminish co-responsibility and cooperation with the laity. Even more problematic, it diminishes the meaning of being one church. Why do we say this? The *Catechism of the Catholic Church* states there is a common priesthood of the baptized and that "all the faithful participate, 'each in its own proper way in the one priesthood of Christ.' "[12] This implied co-responsibility is not just a convenience of ministry; it's essential to the meaning of being one priesthood and Church. Without a doubt, our priesthood is theologically different from the priesthood of the laity. However, it should never be so different that it creates a wall between us and everyone else, a reality that would take the heart out of working together.

When we summarize all the reasons priests leave active ministry, one comes to the forefront over and over: purpose! It can be the loss of purpose, the wrong purpose, an unclear and undefined purpose, or a doubtful purpose. These challenges to our purpose lead us to ask what more we need to do to keep it correct, clear, strong, and committed. To begin with, we need to take the statistics on our priesthood more seriously and ask how we can avoid adding to the list of priests who have left. We need also to remember the adage "There but for the grace of God go I."

According to the Congregation for Clergy, 70,000 priests worldwide resigned between 1964 and 2004. Between 2000 and 2004 alone, we lost 11,210 priests. This is an extremely large number of priests when compared with the decades that preceded 1964. As large as this number is, most sociologists would agree that it's low because it does not reflect those who left without resigning. The bleeding may not be as heavy as it has been, but it will continue to happen. How, then, can we avoid contributing to these numbers? Before answering this question, an observation is in order. When I use the word "we," I mean just that. Maintaining our priestly vocation should not be interpreted as a rugged, Spartan individualistic effort!

A spiritual director once counseled us as seminarians to think seriously through what it means to be a servant to others. "Some of us feel that priesthood is an unqualified total giving of ourselves. This is false!" he would thunder. "We must remember that we not only give support, but also need it." I don't believe any of us really enjoys entering the new era of the "lone ranger priest." And yet, if we take a long-range view of it, it does contain a blessing in disguise; that is, it encourages us to mirror our one priesthood in baptism and reach out to our laity for support.

I will never forget that spiritual director telling us, "In the past, the support of the laity was frowned on because we were considered 'a person set apart.' " He wasn't referring to recluses or clerical enclaves. He meant parish priests. Then he hastened to add: "To stay spiritually and physically healthy implies we humbly admit the need for support—yes, support from the laity! Read the Bible and see how often Christ was supported by others!"

Returning now to the question we have posed—how to keep our purpose clear and avoid losing our vocation—let's listen to the wisdom of the ages on this point. The renowned theologian Father Romano Guardini gives us an excellent description of courage and its implications for keeping our purpose clear and strong. "Courage," he states, "is the confidence required for living with a view to the future, for acting, building, assuming responsibilities and forming ties. For, in spite of our precautions, the future is in each case the unknown. But living means advancing into this unknown region, which may lie before us like chaos into which we must venture. Here everyone must make the venture in the confidence that the future is not chaos or a totally strange thing. Rather, his own character, the ordering power within him, will make a way so that it is really his own future into which he moves."[13]

Note how Guardini directs us to be assertive and adventuresome. In counseling us to advance into unknown regions, he is motivating us to reach out. Interestingly, "reaching out" is the Latin meaning of the word "purpose." Reading between the lines, we learn that Guardini is prompting us to expand our purpose, to will new meanings, to avoid the status quo. We are being reminded that we are a pilgrim church that is forever marching to a new land.

The revered spiritual writer Thomas Merton would counsel us to be realistic about practicing purposefulness. From his own experience, he learned that keeping it clear is not easy. "I see more and more that my understanding of myself and of my life has always been most inadequate. Now that I want more than ever to see, I realize how difficult it is."[14] From Merton's reflection we learn that remaining purposeful is like remaining sinless. We need to expect dark moments of failure mixed with the life-giving light of certainty. To remain purposeful requires continuous conversions of heart.

Cardinal Carlo Martini pointed us to St. Paul and encouraged us to reflect on what strengthened Paul's purposefulness amidst difficult times with the Corinthians. "In spite of these travails I [Martini] was struck by the 'extreme confidence in his [Paul's] own charism' . . . We find a man who is absolutely certain that everything around him may crack but not his own charism. Even when he gives vent to his sufferings most forcefully, he emerges absolutely certain of the charism that has been given to him . . . This is impressive, because his troubles could have made him weaken and become afraid. They might have made him wonder: Is this really my charism? Is it that strong? Must I trust it to last?"[15] In St. Paul, we find the epitome of keeping our purpose clear: to be forever reflecting on our God-given gifts. The clearer we are about these graces, the firmer will be our priestly heart. The more grateful we are for them, the greater the possibility of them carrying the day for us.

Finally, we turn to Teresa of Ávila and her spiritual work *The Interior Castle*. In it she counsels us, "Self-knowledge is the one set of rooms in which we may tarry for as long as we like. It is here that the preparation for the journey to God is accomplished."[16]

There is a species of person called a
"Modern Churchman" who draws the full
salary of a beneficed clergyman and need
not commit himself to any religious belief.[17]
EVELYN WAUGH (1903–1966), BRITISH NOVELIST

2

RESISTING RESENTMENT, CAREERISM, AND CLERICALISM

WHAT ARE THE most serious foes that can take the heart out of our priesthood? Without a doubt, resentment, careerism, and clericalism endanger our priestly heart most. Why do I say this? My choice of resentment comes from a phenomenon I experience repeatedly in conducting priest retreats and days of recollection, as well as preaching homilies to groups of priests. Whenever resentment is mentioned, the audience responds with affirmative nods. Grudges and bitterness are difficult to get over.

Countering resentment is especially important for our priesthood because resentment is the direct antithesis of kindness. Years ago, sociologist Father Andrew Greeley surveyed parishioners, asking them to identify the quality a priest should possess most. As much as being a good homilist, organizer, counselor, and educator are qualities desired by parishioners, being a "kind priest" was the quality that ranked first.

Careerism is singled out because it is a natural driving force in all institutions. It can energize us for doing good, or it can cause us to be self-centered. It also plays strongly to the male mystique.

Clericalism is an occupational hazard that accompanies our privileged role. It is easy to fall prey to elitism, which is the basis of clericalism.

Why is an affirmative nod common when resentment is mentioned? It is because we know how easy it is to become bitter. No one is exempt when it comes to carrying a grudge. The fact that resentment is so pervasive shouldn't amaze us. Just look at the Bible. Cain resents Abel. Joseph is resented by his brothers. Saul resents David, and David's wife resents his dancing before the Ark. In the New Testament the Pharisees, scribes, and Sadducees resent Christ, and Judas resents the man who loved him.

The story of the hired laborer in the Gospel portrays the power that resentment holds for suddenly turning a bright and joyful event into a dark and bitter one. In that story, we hear that early one morning the owner of a vineyard hires an unemployed laborer. Thanks to this new job, the laborer is now promised a paycheck, and more importantly, is given the privilege of feeling the pride and self-respect that comes with employment. What a wonderful way to start the day! At around noon, another unemployed man is hired, and later on yet another is employed. At the end of the day all are paid the same exact wage. Even though the man hired first receives a just wage, he becomes indignant at what he perceives as an unfair payment system. He should have been happy at having any work at all. If he had done a good day's work, it should have given him an added sense of accomplishment. Most of all, he has a paycheck. And yet, this isn't enough. Resentment transforms him into a bitter person.

The word "resentment" denotes being at war within oneself or against another. Being resentful often raises malicious thoughts such as "I deserve better than what I am receiving" or "Don't let them get away with that!" or "Who do they think they are dealing with, a fool?" At other times resentment prompts us to think, "The world is against me, don't ever forget it!" On this last sentiment, the French philosopher Voltaire would comment, "Never having been able to succeed in the world, he took his revenge by speaking ill of it."

Revenge doesn't always follow resentment, but lifelong grudges can. As a child, I would sometimes voice my resentments repeatedly. The third time around my mother would say to me, "That's an old *canzone*—an old song. Turn over the record and let life begin anew!" Despite knowing that deep-seated resentments are wrong, it is difficult to turn over that record. The word "bitterness" comes from the word "bite." When we are bitten we are injured, and like an injured beast, we retaliate.

In the Spanish version of the Benedictus, we find the phrase *sombra de muerte*, the cloud of darkness that hung over the world until Christ, the Light of the World, came to dispel it. Resentments are dark clouds that destroy our ability to smile and be ourselves.

In *Hearts That We Broke Long Ago*, Canadian writer Merle Shain sums up the dreadful effects resentment has on us. "Until one forgives, life is governed by an endless cycle of resentments and retaliations, and we spend our days scratching at the scabs of the wounds that we sustained long ago instead of letting them dry up and disappear. There is no way to hate another that does not cost the hater, no way to remain unforgiving without maiming yourself, because undissolved anger shutters through the body of the person who cannot forgive."[18]

What are some of the major reasons for resentment in our priesthood? They may be:

- An uncommunicative bishop or superior
- The feeling of being unrecognized, misunderstood, or passed over
- Not receiving a parish or position we felt we deserved
- Priests who leave and "desert" us, or who have embarrassed us by unpriestly behavior
- Uncooperative parishioners
- Priests who are forever tearing down the Church and the priesthood
- Conservatives, if we are liberal, and liberals, if we are conservative
- Married men from other denominations being allowed to become priests while talk of a married priesthood is off-limits
- International priests within our ranks, or being an international priest who feels unaccepted
- The censuring of seemingly honest theologians
- Poor health
- The slow pace of renewal, and at times, its reversal
- Decrees from Rome that seem to be insensitive to the American culture

The laundry list of woes is endless. Harboring resentments is one thing; being on the receiving end of them is yet another.

A friend who became a vicar general once confided, "The guys used to like me before I received this position, and I really cherished that camaraderie. But once you're raised above peers, it's interesting how the level of resentment toward you also rises." As he told me this, I could hear the crowds saying of Jesus, "Is not this the carpenter's son?" (Matthew 13:55). How very difficult it is to see someone from among our ranks elevated!

Would that resentments such as these were the only ones badgering our priesthood. Unfortunately, resentment has several levels and the higher the level, the more difficult it is to expunge.

At the moment, the level of resentment over the handling of sexual abuse cases still remains high. Several priests have confided that their respect for the Church has diminished substantially because of the manner in which sexual abuse scandals were handled. One priest raged, "The idea of three strikes and you are out is so secularly American, and ever so divorced from Christian theology. The religious orders handled them much better."

It is true that religious orders were under the same heavy pressure as were our bishops. And yet from all outward appearances, they seemed to have been better balanced when handling the problem of sexual abuse among their ranks. Take, for example, the response made by Father Ted Keating, SM, who at the time was the executive director of the Conference of Major Superiors of Men (CMSM), regarding the handling of these men. "Whether he's sick, or in prison, or charged with something, he's still a member of the family, and we take care of him and watch out for him, even though we would not tolerate what he did in any way and will hold him accountable for his behaviors."[19]

The CMSM statement echoes the age-old belief *Tu es sacerdos in aeternum,* and suggests the image of the good shepherd seeking the lost sheep. It not only reflects the Good Shepherd, but it also contains a quality of love that is seldom mentioned— fraternal correction, i.e., if there is priestly misconduct, it is to be corrected immediately. Tough love is to be applied. By no means did religious orders look the other way. Like the bishops, they disciplined their priests severely, but most of them didn't throw their priests out onto the street.

In addition to the reasons why resentment is difficult to curtail, allow me to recall two personal experiences that get to the heart of this difficulty.

In Italian, we have the phrase *non si preoccupare,* loosely translated "Don't worry" or "Don't let something grip you to the point that it takes possession of you." This is extremely difficult to practice. Resentments penetrate deep into our entire being, and once there, recycle themselves, mutate, and grow stronger.

During my ministerial life, I have counseled women whose marriages had been annulled. In the course of our conversations, they often spoke openly about their ex-husbands. Listening between the lines, I could see they still loved them. Every time I have gently said, "You still love him, don't you?" tears welled up and the head bowed, indicating "yes."

When we are deeply touched by another, whether it is through love, or a love betrayed, the heart is pierced. No matter how much the mind may say, "Forget it and let life begin anew," it is very difficult to convince an afflicted heart. I will never forget watching Pietro Mascagni's opera *Cavalleria Rusticana* with my mother. The opening scene begins with a heartbroken woman crying profusely for a man she loves. He, on the other hand, could not care less about her. As she became more passionate, I remember that I turned to my mother and said, "He's a bum; throw the bum out and your problems will be over." Mom turned to me and just said, "It doesn't go that way!"

What might be a good lesson in combating resentment? The revered theologian Karl Rahner would remind us, "Remember we are less than perfect!" One of the major blocks to curing resentments is self-righteousness, the feeling that we are above reproach and hence don't deserve affliction. In these cases, Rahner would tell us to remember that as we have been injured by others, so too have we injured others. Once we humbly admit this, it is easier to let go of resentments.

The opposite of resentment is the foremost virtue our laity desire in us: kindness. Kindness is being well disposed toward oneself and life. When we model it in our daily lives, it becomes our best antidote for combating resentment. Cardinal John Henry Newman's description of a gentleman captures this model par excellence.

> A gentleman is mainly occupied in merely removing the obstacles which hinder the free and unembarrassed action of those about him. The true gentleman in like manner carefully avoids whatever may cause a jar or jolt in the minds of those with whom he is cast; all clashing of opinion, or collision of feelings, all restraint, or suspicion, or gloom, or resentment; his great concern being to make everyone at their ease and at home. He has eyes on all his company; he is tender toward the bashful, gentle toward the distant, and merciful toward the absurd; he can recollect to whom he is speaking; he guards against unseasonable allusions, or topics which may irritate; he is seldom prominent in conversation, and never wearisome. He makes light of favors while he

does them, and seems to be receiving when he is conferring. He never speaks of himself except when compelled, never defends himself by a mere retort, he has no ears for slander or gossip, is scrupulous in imputing motives to those who interfere with him, and interprets everything for the best. He is never mean or little in disputes, never takes unfair advantage, never mistakes personalities or sharp sayings for arguments, or insinuates evil which he dare not say out. From a long sighted prudence, he observes the maxim of the ancient sage, that we should ever conduct ourselves toward our enemy as if he were one day to be our friend.[20]

Note how Newman reminds us to choose our words well and to make them as melodious as possible. Interestingly, Cicero in his treatise *On Duty* advises his son Marcus to practice melodious speech because friendships come much easier when speech fits to the liking of the listener. The presence or absence of melodious speech is an excellent indicator of our disposition. When resentment takes hold of us, it is common for our speech to become strident, cold, and inhuman.

In counseling us to make everyone at ease and at home, Newman is actually addressing civility. Ironically, the word civility denotes home. When I first learned this, I couldn't connect with it. Then it dawned on me that civility is the art of making people feel at home.

In encouraging us to be merciful toward the absurd, Newman addresses the heart. The word "mercy" in Latin is *misericordia*, which means to possess a heart that feels pity. In Newman's definition of a gentleman, we have the perfect formula for kindness and the priestly heart expected by those we serve.

Turning now to the second major foe of our priesthood, we need to ask why careerism is named. Even though Pope

Benedict XVI could have chosen other topics more appropriate to the occasion, his homily to the first priests he ordained as pope contained a reflection on careerism. "Carreerism," he said, "is the attempt to get ahead, to gain a position through the church: to make use of and not to serve."[21] In these words, we can hear the psalmist in Psalm 131 pray:

> Oh Lord, my heart is not lifted up,
>   my eyes are not raised too high;
> I do not occupy myself with things
>   too great and too marvelous for me.
> But I have calmed and quieted my soul,
>   like a weaned child with its mother;
>   my soul is like the weaned child that is
>   with me.
> O Israel, hope in the Lord
>   from this time on and forevermore.
>
> (Psalm 131:1–3)

The psalm teaches us that an inordinate desire for self-advancement is undesirable, and those who successfully avoid the temptation are blessed with a peaceful soul.

The opposite of a careerist, Benedict points out, is a shepherd who knows his or her sheep, cares for them, and is willing to give his or her life for them. This theme of caring for others can be traced to Pope Benedict's classic work *The Introduction to Christianity*, in which he points us to the principle of the preposition "for." He writes: "Because Christian faith demands the individual, but wants him for the whole and not for himself, the really basic law of Christian existence is expressed in the preposition 'For.' . . . That is why in the chief Christian sacrament, which forms the center of Christian worship, the existence of Jesus Christ is explained as existence 'for the many', 'for you', as an open existence which makes possible and creates the communication of all between one another through communication in him."[22]

During the Vietnam War, a reporter asked a native of that country, "Why are your people embracing Communism when you are traditionally Christian?" The man replied, "Because Christians aren't very Christian! They are more interested in themselves than being for others." The Christian principle of the preposition "for" was missing.

The reasons for avoiding careerism remind me of a true story that ended sadly. Immediately after the installation of a new archbishop of a large archdiocese, two powerful monsignors, who were known for running the diocese, lost their diocesan positions and were assigned to well-to-do parishes. Within a year both died of heart attacks. Only God knows why they were taken. The news of their deaths, however, left many of us wondering whether they envisioned their careers as somehow over, and died as a consequence. In cases like this, we learn how easy it is to become immersed in careerism and to twist the principle "for." Instead of being for others we become for ourselves.

When I mentioned Pope Benedict's homily on careerism to a marine general, he said, "I would really like a copy of it. This is one of our biggest problems in the corps. Too many men and women are entering with the idea of making it a personal career. In doing this, they are losing sight of our motto, *Semper Fidelis*. In pledging faithfulness to the corps, a marine dedicates himself or herself to others, not to personal gain."

At the dedication of the new Marine Museum at Quantico, Virginia, Jim Lehrer of the *Lehrer News Hour* gave a keynote speech that deepens the meaning of the "for" preposition.

> It's about the shared experience and the shared knowledge that comes from being a U.S. Marine, such as knowing that you are only as strong and as safe as the person on your right and on your left; that a well-trained and

motivated human being can accomplish almost anything; that being pushed to do your very best is a godsend; that an order is an order, a duty is a duty, that responsibility goes down the chain of command, as well as up, as do loyalty and respect; that leadership can be taught, so can bearing, discipline and honor; that "follow me" really does mean "follow me"; and that *Semper Fidelis* really does mean "always faithful"; and that the Marines hymn is so much more than just a song . . . When Marines stand for or sing the Marine's hymn, . . . it's never for ourselves personally. It's always for Marines who went before us, with us, and after us, first and foremost for those who gave their lives, their health, their everything . . .[23]

The Marine spirit described by Jim Lehrer is the direct antithesis of careerism. Careerism has an uncanny way of making us forget we belong to a corps of men and women who "went before us, are with us, and will come after us."

Careerism is part of life and it is often mistaken for magnanimity. What does magnanimity, which encourages us to utilize our gifts to the fullest, have to say about careerism? How do we interpret St. Thomas Aquinas when he tells us, "It belongs to magnificence to intend doing great work with a broad and noble purpose in mind"? How do we accomplish great work without falling into careerism? Where do we draw the line?

Early on in his career, one of this country's founding fathers, John Adams, faced this same question. The Congress then, as now, was made up of some overachievers and men with inflated egos. In realizing this, Adams believed that a strong sense of duty was the best antidote to careerism. Duty directs us away from ourselves and toward the task at hand.

The ancient Greek poet Homer tells us that the mark of the noble man is a sense of duty. A man is judged and proud to be judged by a severe standard—the standard of duty. How then do we not mistake careerism for magnanimity? By cultivating a noble sense of duty that is forever asking, "What is in it for those I am serving?"

Before leaving these noble principles, it cannot be stated too strongly that the line between magnanimity and careerism is very thin, and is easy to cross.

Let's turn to another foe to our priesthood that is closely connected to careerism: clericalism. How does this come about and what are its signs? Throughout my priesthood—and no doubt in the lives of all priests—it is often the case that we are seated in prominent positions at public events or family functions. In such circumstances, it can become easy to expect this as a part of the priesthood. It is ever so easy to enjoy elitism and the feeling of being a part of the privileged class. In *Spoils of the Kingdom*, Anson Shupe addresses the ins and outs of our privileged class status. "There is an almost inevitable tendency in religious groups, unless they rigorously eschew both institutionalization and the cultivation of hierarchy, to regress from the spiritual equality of laity and clergy toward oligarchy, that is, political control of the many by the few."[24] Quoting Belgian sociologist Robert Michels, Shupe spells out the reasons behind oligarchy, which can easily lead to clericalism in our case.

> First, there is the reality of sheer population density, which renders direct democracy impossible, hence gradually requiring at a minimum a republican, or representative, system of governance. Second, there is the unavoidable "apathy" of most citizens/members whose energies and time are typically consumed by mundane obligations of family, work, leisure, and rest. Third, there is the

inevitability of growing elites' or representatives' self-interests, which include indulgence in the "perks" of power: exclusive knowledge, personal aggrandizement; and controlling client, patient, constituent, or congregant awareness of elite behavior.[25]

We learn from Shupe that governance, by its nature, creates elite groups. This happens because we are too busy keeping ourselves together and tend to leave certain business to others who are considered competent. As often happens with elitism, perks are expected. When applied to clericalism, we learn how easy it is to succumb to it because of our elite position. People are willing to concede power to us because of our status. Once on this level, there is the ever-present temptation to indulge oneself in its power and to cultivate—consciously or unconsciously—a sense of entitlement. Power does corrupt!

In his book *Clericalism: The Death of Priesthood*, George B. Wilson, sj, paints some of the most prominent pictures of clerical attitudes.

- "Because I belong to the clergy I am automatically credible. I don't have to earn my credibility by my performance."

- "People use a special title in addressing me, so I must be something special."

- "The laity accept these manifestations of privilege, so they must be deserved."

- "We deserve any privilege the laity seem to want to give us."

- "We are special. Who are 'they' to judge us?"

- "If you criticize our profession you are disrespecting us as persons. We do not allow outsiders (or insiders) to criticize anyone in our guild."

- "Protecting our image is more important than confronting the situation. If someone blows the whistle on us we will deflect the question and attack the messenger."

- "If we ignore what people are saying, we won't have to change anything."

- "It takes special knowledge and training to become certified. The matters we deal with are beyond the comprehension of the laity."

- "We know what is important in the life of the laity. We don't have to experience it ourselves to give them advice on what to do about it."

- "We don't have to be accountable to the laity. We are their shepherds."

- "I have been ordained. That gives me all I need for my flock. I don't need anything from the other guys tending their flocks."

- "By ordination I enjoy all the gifts the faithful need; I don't have to be dependent on the gifts of others."

- "Keep the voices isolated from one another and they'll never know their potentiality. Divide—and conquer."[26]

Clericalism, resentment, and careerism will always be with us. In the movie *Ben Hur*, there is a scene well worth recalling. It can help us avoid succumbing to these three foes of our priesthood. After Ben Hur has vanquished his rival Marcellus in a furious chariot race, he is crowned the victor by the emperor. Within minutes after this, the stadium becomes eerily quiet. The crowds are gone and there is no one left to vanquish. One senses the emptiness of it all. I recall a woman once saying to me, "That scene reflects a humbling fact of life. Once all its rush, cheering, and exaltation are over and nothing remains but silence, what ultimately have we achieved?" To this we add, "And what is our vocation ultimately about?"

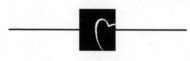

*He prays well who is so absorbed with God
that he does not know he is praying.*

FRANCIS DE SALES (1567–1622)

3

Refining the Habit of Contemplation

I couldn't have asked for a better day: perfect weather, an ideal setting, and standing shoulder to shoulder with a spirited group of healthy marathoners! At the sound of the gun, we tore down a steep hill that wound through an enchanting wooded area. Six minutes into the race someone shouted, "Our first mile was 6.6 minutes." Suddenly I felt as if I had been caught up in a stampede. I thought, "I'm not watching my pace; if I maintain this speed, I will never finish."

We often feel very much like that in our ministry. We forever are running at a fast clip. We get caught up without realizing the speed we are going. No doubt its exhilaration is intoxicating, and no doubt we can justify our pace of life on the grounds that we are working ourselves to death for the Kingdom of God. Over the years I have known priests who lived this philosophy. And over those same years I saw a very high number burn out when they got swallowed up by a hyperactive world, to the neglect of their contemplative life. In her memoirs, Anne Morrow Lindbergh addresses one of the sad results of this neglect: "We seem so frightened of being alone that we never let it happen . . . We choke the space with continuous music, chatter, and companionship to which we do not even listen. It is simply there to fill the vacuum. When the noise stops there is no inner music to take its place."[27] Choked by hyperactivity, we lose a sense of inner harmony and its restorative powers.

The renowned psychologist Erich Fromm tells us that the loss of inner harmony also leaves the door open to psychological problems. He contends that if we are deprived of daily stimulation for any length of time, many of us will not be able to endure it and will need psychological help. The need for stimulation and continuous activity is simply part of the human condition. It is also why many people find it very difficult to practice its antithesis: contemplation. As a society, we tend to mirror our stampeding culture and its addiction to hyperactivity. Unfortunately, this often results in becoming shallow, lacking substance, and, in our case, depriving our priestly heart of its greatest source of energy. Romano Guardini foresaw that our age would become more and more hyperactive. In his book *Power and Responsibility*, he gives us a good insight into the damage this inflicts on us, and how to counteract it. "All around us we see activity, organization, operations of every possible type; but what directs them? An inwardness no longer really at home with itself. An 'interiority' too superficial to contact the truth lying at life's center, which no longer reaches the essential and everlasting, but remains somewhere just under the skin-level of the provisional and the fortuitous."[28]

And what does Guardini suggest is our best means for cultivating a wholesome interiority? "Before all else, then, man's depths must be reawakened. His life must again include times, his day moments of stillness in which he collects himself, spreads out before his heart the problems which have stirred him during the day. In a word, man must learn again to meditate and to pray."[29]

During a meeting at St. Meinrad's Abbey in Saint Meinrad, Indiana, Rabbi Arthur Hertzberg echoed Guardini's sentiments and insights. In wondering about the merits of contemplation and what seminarians, once ordained, will bring to the world, Hertzberg also prompts us to ponder the merits of contemplation in a world of hyperactivity and what we who are ordained bring to the world.

> The men of religion will find the world soon enough, for it beats insistently upon everybody. The question remains: What will they bring to the world out of the transforming power of their faith? We are talking very much today of bringing religion into the world, but after that glittering proposition is stated I hear little agreement on what the message to be brought ought to be. I sat at St. Meinrad and wondered whether it would not be better for at least some men to make it their vocation to keep examining this world of ours while remaining strongly rooted in a community of worship and contemplation. Religion and the world are, by their very nature, in tension. The urges to contemplation and action are the reflections of this tension in the lives of men. Precisely because we are all so busy in action, or in feeling guilty that we are not active enough, St. Meinrad reminded me that Moses was not

always in the midst of affairs in the camp of
the Jews. He was most useful to them and most
transforming of them after he had ascended
Mount Sinai and was alone with God for forty
days.[30]

Lindbergh, Fromm, Guardini, and Hertzberg address a
monumental challenge confronting today's priesthood: how to
place an accent on contemplation in our daily lives and make
it the most valued tool we possess for enriching our ministry.
It may be argued that we do pray and practice contemplation
already, so why be so emphatic about it? Sad to say, the major
criticism against us these days is a lack of reflectiveness that
leads to a lack of substance. The richness of the gospel we
champion isn't surfacing in our lives and ministry as it should.
Studies repeatedly reveal that our homilies could use much
more substance. We often are criticized for not taking time to
think them through at a deeper level. The same criticism holds
for our liturgies, sacramental life, and catechesis. Too often
they lack inspiring imagination and an attractive sacredness
that only contemplation can create.

Pope Paul VI implies as much in the encyclical *Evangelii
Nuntiandi*. In its opening paragraphs he asks, "To what extent
and in what way is that evangelical force capable of really
transforming the people of this century? What methods should
be followed in order that the power of the Gospel may have its
effect? Basically, these inquiries make explicit the fundamental
question that the Church is asking herself today and which
may be expressed in the following terms: after the Council and
thanks to the Council, which was a time given her by God, at
this turning-point of history, does the Church or does she not
find herself better equipped to proclaim the Gospel and to put
it into people's hearts with conviction, freedom of spirit and
effectiveness?"[31] It is no stretch of the imagination to say that
Pope Paul VI is calling for a more contemplative evangelization

that carries a punch. His questions are disturbing, but they are not meant to be negative. Rather, he is prompting us to bring the powers of contemplation to bear on our thinking. Along this line of thought, Franklin D. Roosevelt once said, "Concentration is the secret of our strength."

What exactly is contemplation, and what might be good examples of it in practice? Pope John Paul II is one good example. After the pope's death, Cardinal Theodore McCarrick recalled one of his most memorable experiences with him. As John Paul II entered a chapel, he fell to his knees in prayer. "It was an awesome moment like no other I encountered," recalls McCarrick. "The pope went into deep prayer and was all there with God. Sensing its solemnity, I slipped behind a pillar so as not to disturb the moment."[32]

In one of my retreats I used this example of Pope John Paul II. After one of the sessions, a priest knocked on my door and asked to talk with me. I first thought he wanted some counseling or to go to confession. I was wrong. What he wanted to talk about was his experience with Pope John Paul II when he was in Poland. "I remember a camping trip I took with Karol Wojtyla, who was a bishop then," he told me. "During one afternoon when I wanted to ask him a question, I found him sitting under a tree reading his breviary. I approached him and asked my question, but he seemed not to hear it. Suddenly I realized he was in deep contemplation. I know exactly what you meant when you shared Cardinal McCarrick's story!"

Church commentators have often pointed to the pope's physical fitness and Spartan Polish background as reasons for his being able to weather debilitating medical problems. But were these the principal reasons for his strength, or was it the depth of contemplation he reached and the strength this generated?

Interestingly, the entrance to the U.S. Supreme Court in Washington, D.C., has a striking symbol of the contemplation that is required in the process of creating just laws. A Romanesque statute of a woman holding a child greets visitors as they ascend the court's steps. Her head and eyes are bowed as if she is in pain. Actually, she is *The Contemplation of Justice*. When we look closely, we see that the boy in her lap is holding the scales of justice. *The Contemplation of Justice* symbolizes the rudiments of contemplation: withdrawal from the distractions of everyday activities in order to gain clarity of interior vision. She is the personification of quietness plumbing the depths of justice. Contemplation here is seen as stillness, which Romano Guardini defines as "a collected, total presence; a being 'all there,' receptive, alert, ready. It is when the soul abandons the restlessness of purposeful activity."[33]

The philosopher Josef Pieper would concur and take us even deeper into the meaning of contemplation as a means of gazing upon and submitting to that which we see. In contemplation, we allow ourselves to be caught up in the grasp of that upon which we look. Interestingly, Pieper sees contemplation as the basis of leisure and of a true celebration of life. When I first pondered these notions, I had difficulty envisioning "being all there," "collected," "gazing," and "receptivity." What especially stumped me was trying to understand how contemplation and celebrating life complemented each other.

I stumbled on the answer one afternoon while visiting a museum on our mall in Washington, D.C. On exhibit was a large wall-sized photo of an exquisite synagogue in Detroit. Its interior was awesome: rich blues, golds, reds, and the deep warmth of mahogany wood. The more I gazed upon it, the more I became united to it, and the more I became one with it, the more it energized me. As I walked home, I said to myself, "That was a rich experience; it made my day!" Then, "Ah," I thought, "this is what Pieper means by celebration!" I realized that the most memorable celebrations I have experienced have been heartfelt moments of sharing ideas, aspirations, and dreams with close friends. We became as one. It can rightly be said that these were sacramental moments. We must wonder if ecstatic moments like this are a tiny glimpse of what the Beatific Vision will be like: a total abandonment of restless activity that frees us to be one with God—a sacramental eternity?

Calmness is closely related to contemplation. In Greek "calm" means "the heat of the day," suggesting the image of coming out of the pounding sun and getting away from that which wears on us. Seen another way, calmness lays the groundwork for contemplation by urging us to remove ourselves from our hyperactive work in order to maintain the composure needed to be effective.

Where might we turn for help in rededicating ourselves to our contemplative powers? Who or what might give us the jumpstart we need to refurbish it? I believe retreats are one good opportunity for accomplishing this—that is, if we make them properly. Most retreat settings are located in beautiful, secluded hideaways. Retreats are made for the very purpose of praying, contemplating, and leaving behind restless activity.

As wonderful as retreats are, many of us fall short when it comes to leaving restless activity behind. Why? Perhaps it is through no fault of our own. We usually begin retreats on the heels of frenzied activities. It is a fact of nature that calmness doesn't kick in immediately the moment we get away from our hectic work. It takes time to leave our activities behind and just to let go. If we were to make a thirty-day retreat, getting into its spirit would be easier to accomplish. However, most of us don't have this luxury. Another reason our retreats fall short may be the expectation that they will serve as an opportunity for recreation and camaraderie, rather than a time for silence and serious reflection.

Whatever the reasons, sad to say, many retreats aren't true celebrations, according to Pieper's conception of celebration.

We don't get into a gazing-being-all-there spirit. More often than not, we are still "all there" back at the parish.

As a retreat master, I often wonder whether our retreats would be more beneficial if, first and foremost, we made the cultivation of calmness a daily habit. Pope John XXIII was a good example of this. As he prepared for bed he would pray: "Lord, I have done all I can for the day. It's now time for you to take over. Good night." As busy as his schedule was, Pope John knew how to leave it all behind him. He practiced the saintly spiritual principle of total abandonment to God.

Having now addressed the momentous need for contemplation, we need to turn to its awesome powers. I believe that one reason contemplation is often neglected is because we don't truly cherish its powers.

While competing in a Chicago triathlon I accidentally learned of a power of contemplation few of us consider: its enormous ability to renew our courage and our physical strength. The moment the starting horn is sounded, triathletes go into a frenzy of motion. The most frightening event in a triathlon is the mile swim that begins the race. What makes it nerve-racking is that the triathlete is competing with fifty or more swimmers who are constantly bumping into one other or swimming over one another in deep water. One triathlon in which I competed was especially frightening because of cold, rough water. One minute the swimmers around me were visible; the next moment they were lost to sight in high swells. Not only this, but a number of shivering, disoriented swimmers began to panic and call for help. That same panic hit me, leaving me unnerved and terrified. I remember thinking to myself, "This is how people can drown in a matter of minutes." For some unknown reason I was able to go within myself, become still and recollected, and be all there. Once into this contemplative mood, I focused on relaxing and not fighting the water. Suddenly inner calmness and renewed vigor enveloped me. I was astonished how I had lost nerve—my courage—and felt powerless one moment, and the next moment I was up to full strength. Until that incident, I never realized the awesome power contemplation contains for regaining our nerve and courage, and renewing our physical energy.

Needless to say, when the race was over I celebrated. To my amazement, the thing I cherished most was my almost instinctive ability to attain that state of contemplative awareness, and thus draw on my own courage and strength to over come fear and panic. It was very much like the unitive feeling I experienced in being one with the picture of the synagogue.

Self-possession is another one of contemplation's powers. My book *The Promise of Virtue* contains a chapter on silence. When I began writing about silence, I remember taking a bike ride and thinking, "I really don't fully understand this virtue. After years of practicing silence in the seminary and throughout my whole life, I still feel inadequate in writing about it." But then it occurred to me that I know more about the powers of silence than I was giving myself credit for. All I needed to do was to revisit the life of Christ through the eyes of silence. This refection, in turn, led me to re-examine the trial of Christ before Pilate.

In some accounts of the trial, the one thing that stands out most is Christ's silence. In fact, one scripture scholar told me that some scholars feel that Christ never uttered a word during the trial. My reflections on Christ's trial started with his being arrested, scourged, mocked, and then led to Pilate for trial.

"When morning came, all the chief priests and the elders of the people conferred together against Jesus in order to bring about his death. They bound him, led him away, and handed him over to Pilate the governor" (Matthew 27:1–2). Christ finds himself bound like a common prisoner and derided by the very persons who should have been the first to comprehend who he was. This is irony at its worst, and when we are victims of it we want to shout to the heavens for justice. But Christ does not shout; he hardly murmurs a word. Rather, he humbly stands before Pilate, who asks, "Are you the king of the Jews?" The question is legitimate and Christ answers, "You say so." This disturbs the chief priests and elders who are out to misconstrue his words and actions in order to condemn him. Christ is not hurt so much by their false accusations as he is by seeing how their jealousy has eaten away at the very dignity they received from his Father. They are men intent on killing him, men who have lost sight of who they are.

Then Pilate says to him, "Don't you hear how many things they are accusing you of?" But he does not answer Pilate one word, and the governor is greatly amazed. But why be amazed? Could it be that Pilate senses in Christ a patient man who reflects the saying, "Through patience a man possesses his soul"? Does Christ's stillness cause Pilate to realize he is in the presence of one greater than himself and those who accuse Christ? Is the force of Christ's silence so powerful that Pilate cannot but be amazed by its magnitude? I believe we can truly answer yes to each of these questions. In saying yes, we also say yes to the self-possession Christ mirrored because of his practice of prayer and contemplation.

Having now reflected on the powers of contemplation, we need to ask a practical question: How do we cultivate it in our rushed and hectic environments? I believe our age is calling for a new creativity in finding ways to practice contemplation amidst our busy daily schedules. On our Web site for The National Institute for the Renewal of the Priesthood[34], we posted a question aimed at surfacing the most imaginative way of staying contemplative. We asked, "How do you maintain your spiritual life amidst a busy daily schedule?" The answers we received were gratifying in that many of us are very creative in balancing our contemplative life with our hectic life. Listen to the following replies we received to see how creative we are.

One priest told us, "To the specifics regarding sustaining ingredients to a priestly spirituality, don't forget *places*. For example, my car is an important place for me to go to pray. No phones. No interruptions. My car is important. Do priests have other holy/common places? I'm an old English teacher. Your examples list persons and things [that help spirituality]. But a noun like 'spirituality' could use a *place* in translation, too."

Another priest responded, "I tried to tell my associate that the forty-minute trip to Queen of Heaven Cemetery wouldn't be so bad if he used his car as a chapel. I do, at least sometimes."

A priest who is a runner said, "Running alone has a unique stillness about it, especially if you are running through a wooded area. For me, it is the perfect place to collect myself and contemplate God's plan for me. It is my chapel."

A priest once told me that he needed a push to get into a contemplative mode. "I will be honest with you," he said, "I'm not a contemplative guy. In fact, I sort of run from it because I don't particularly enjoy silence. I am also afraid of what I might learn if I get too contemplative. It takes a lot to move me into even considering contemplation. Some tell me the movie *Into Great Silence* is well worth seeing, and that it may just be the push I need."

Along this same line of thought, another priest said: "One day a friend gave me a recording of Gregorian chant. As I played its soothing melodies, they reminded me of the seminary and the number of hours I spent in chapel observing silence. Perhaps this was a grace from God telling me to recapture those experiences."

Ironically, I have found the train an excellent place to contemplate. I say "ironically" because the experience of trains and train stations is normally marked by hustle and bustle. Periodically I take the Metroliner from Washington, D.C. to New York City. To my surprise, I learned they have quiet cars. I found that rolling through the countryside and just gazing out the window in silence is the perfect setting for contemplation.

If we look for them, creative means for sharpening our contemplative edge are everywhere. We just need to be creative in seeking them. Take, for example, the practice called "Timeshifting," an approach to life that I learned about while posting books on our Web site. This approach contains a good lesson on how to be "all there" in our ministry. Timeshifting is a practice that encourages us to concentrate on our rhythms to learn what rhythms might need to be shifted. If we are moving too quickly, the goal of Timeshifting is to realize this and shift into a much slower pace. If we find we are wasting a lot of time that could be put to better use by praying, Timeshifting prompts us to turn this around by shifting away from wasted time to time for being with God. Timeshifting is an excellent means for fostering contemplation because it encourages us first to examine the unhealthy rituals into which we have fallen, and then to seek ways of switching to more beneficial rituals. Timeshifting is one of numerous available methods for shifting ourselves away from a hyperactive and sometimes empty life to a more contemplative and enriched life.

One last comment is in order. First and foremost, contemplation must be our means of drawing closer to God. To lose sight of this is to reduce contemplation to just another psychological method of coping with life's challenges. It is true that contemplation is wonderful for increasing our depth, self-possession, calmness, and energy. Contemplation leads us toward a true celebration of life. It is equally true that contemplation is our best line of defense against ineptness, superficiality, mindlessness, and mimicking a society that often tends to be hectic. Truest of all is that contemplation is a spiritual means of making us holier and closer to God.

We are extremely fortunate in this age of busy-ness to have been formed by the sacred tradition of contemplation in our seminary education. The biggest challenge we face—now that we are ordained—is growing in that tradition and keeping our contemplative and prayerful edge sharp.

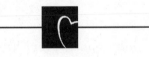

*A spirituality that is prophetic is rooted in
social, economic, and political reality.
One cannot be ignorant of or removed from
the needs, aspirations, movements,
and accomplishments of society
and presume to be prophetic.*

DIANNE BERGANT, CSA

4

Study Is Ministry!

NEVER ACCENT ACTIVE ministry to the point that the life of the mind is neglected! There are four crucial reasons to make ongoing education an essential part of our pastoral ministry. When we let our ongoing education slide, it is easy to slip into feeding pious pap to our people, providing second-rate services, and, simply put, our actions become less meaningful. Worse than this, out-of-date theology, below-par administrative and liturgical services, and superficiality have been known to cause people to leave the Church.

The renowned author and homilist Father Walter Burghardt, SJ, pulls no punches about the importance of keeping up our education: "Unless the Spirit-led ministry of American priests pays high tribute to the life of the mind, unless the majority of Catholic seminaries cultivates intelligence with seriousness and in depth, we risk losing today's masses . . . the educated class."[35]

Even though we may be kind, generous, and always there for our people, it is equally important to provide them the fullness of God's word. Accomplishing this requires that we plumb the word's depths, recast its meaning for our times, and always present it intelligently.

Years ago Washington Theological Union in Washington, D.C. was blessed to have on its faculty the theologian Father Michael Scanlon, osa, who would pound this adage home to seminarians: "Study is ministry!" At first this sounds like an exaggeration. However, one look at the harm we do when we neglect the life of our minds proves how right he is. For example, I have had parents confide in me, "We hope for good homilies at the Sunday Mass, not so much for our benefit, but for our teenage children." A constant weight on their minds is the fear that their children will lose the faith.

No doubt we have heard stories of priests whose thoughtful homilies were responsible for keeping young people close to the sacraments. When we look behind this, it is commonly found that these priests are forever building up their knowledge about youth: their lifestyles, thinking, and what attracts them most. Father Scanlon is so correct in emphasizing that study is ministry, especially ministry to our young people who are the future of the Church.

What do we actually mean when we say we should pay high tribute to the life of the mind? Simply put, it means pursuing ongoing education, study, research, and reading, and seeking out knowledgeable people from whom we can learn. Cardinal John Henry Newman would tell us to cultivate a mind that forever seeks deeper meaning, new insights, and "invests in ideas."[36]

As wonderful as new ideas are, the most important thing in paying high tribute to the mind is that it enables us to be truly prophetic, to practice cutting-edge evangelization, and to address the new challenges of this millennium intelligently! To be prophetic requires that we look at the world around us with the eyes of a sociologist, anthropologist, psychologist, and economist. I am not proposing that we become social scientists, but rather that we see the fruits of their work as essential to our prophetic role. In the *Dictionary of Spirituality*, Dianne Bergant, CSA, gives sage insight into how the social sciences and our prophetic role complement each other.

> A spirituality that is prophetic is rooted in social, economic, and political reality. One cannot be ignorant of or removed from the needs, aspirations, movements, and accomplishments of society and presume to be prophetic. It is within this reality that God is revealed, either reassuring the people of divine compassion and care or warning them of God's indignation and justice. Human history with all its possibilities, challenges, and risks is the matrix within which the reign of God takes shape. Its dynamism and novelty can be neither repressed nor ignored for it mirrors the creativity of God.[37]

In the book *Shaping Catholic Parishes* is the story of lay minister Adam Ruiz, who was challenged by the matrix about which Bergant speaks. "Connecting the real lives of the people with the ministry of the church" is the key, Ruiz says of his work. He "learned firsthand" about the problems people face in his area: "underemployment, cultural shock, language barriers, immigration status, domestic violence, alcoholism, prostitution, parallel society."[38] As commendable as is the ministry of Ruiz and others like him, we need to wonder how much easier and more effective it would be if his firsthand knowledge was aided by social science—if he were able to review some of the studies on underemployment, cultural shock, language barriers, and so on.

A letter I received from a woman who read my syndicated column, "Where Have All the Catholics Gone?", gives us yet another reason to "go to school" to learn about those to whom we minister. She wrote, "The only thing I had to see was the caption 'Where Have All the Catholics Gone?', and it drew me to read your article. I have found a few friends and some acquaintances have left the Catholic Church for other beliefs. For a long time I found myself going to Mass on and off, then not going for over a year because I wasn't getting anything out of the homily. I eventually went back and found a church with a priest that drew crowds for Mass; his secret was he preached about everyday life which everyone could relate to."

In reading this, we have to wonder how many more people would be coming to our parishes if we did our homework better, if we learned about the world in which they live and addressed it as that priest did. Undoubtedly, prophetic gifts are a grace from God. However, they are also best practiced when we do homework on the signs of the times and how they apply to our people. The more we study and know them, the better we can be a *nabi* (a prophet), a man of spirit.

Cultivating the life of the mind has another benefit: it enables us to practice cutting-edge evangelization. In the encyclical *Evangelii Nuntiandi*, Pope Paul VI implores us, "For the church it is a question not only of preaching the Gospel in ever wider geographic areas, . . . but also of affecting and as it were upsetting, through the power of the Gospel, mankind's criteria of judgment, determining values, points of interest, lines of thought, sources of inspiration and models of life, which are in contrast with the Word of God and the plan of salvation."[39]

In advocating that we upset the world's values, Pope Paul VI is calling for the creation of a spiritual tension between the secular world and God's world. He is not advocating tension for tension's sake, but rather a tension that causes people to rethink their life in relation to God's life. But how can we accomplish this realistically? Is it not by becoming as knowledgeable as possible about people's values, beliefs, and mores so that we can challenge them to be better?

Another major benefit of paying high tribute to the mind is the power it gives us to achieve solidarity. Newly arrived immigrants will be, or will stop being, present in our parishes depending on how well we relate to them and create a sense of oneness with them. At the moment, studies reveal that Hispanic young adults as a group are "more religiously disengaged than other Catholic teens, despite the fact that they participate in more personal and family-based spiritual practices and their parents demonstrate greater commitment to their faith than do the white Catholic parents."[40]

When Archbishop—later Cardinal—Pio Laghi was apostolic delegate to the U.S., he gave a talk in which he urged the U.S. bishops to encourage seminarians and priests to go beyond learning modern languages and to study cultural diversity. In reality, he was calling for the broader base of knowledge that is needed if solidarity is to be established with multicultural populations. He was advocating a new holistic model of inculturation requiring several types of knowledge rather than only knowledge of a language.

In Latin, we have two words for knowing, *cognoscere* and *sapere*. *Cognoscere* means to know about someone or something. *Sapere* is much more intimate, meaning we know something or someone in the deepest sense of the word. One thing—more than any other—that is accomplished through education, study, and research for our ministry is this: we can go deeper with our people. The deeper we go, the more realistically we can serve them.

We now need to ask, "How is paying high tribute to the mind perceived in everyday ministry?"

Normally when we envision ongoing education, we're inclined to see it in an academic setting. Today there are priests in these settings as full-time students obtaining degrees for specialized ministry in the Church. There also are priests on sabbaticals refreshing their studies. These two cases are exceptions, and are to be lauded, but they are not very applicable to those of us in daily ministry. What are our best options? If we have access to a university or college, how about becoming a part-time student? Even if we attend part-time for one hour a week, getting away from parochial confines can be a breath of fresh air, and, to boot, it keeps our taste for studies alive. As a newly ordained priest I learned how true this is.

After completing twelve years of seminary training, seven of which were taught in Latin, the last thing I desired was to return to school. I thanked God that the years of attending classes, writing papers, and taking exams were over. Now was the time to put my education to work! Several months into my first parish assignment, this attitude was to change when the director of religious education announced that I was being sent back to school to pursue a degree in religious education on a part-time basis. I remember my disbelief in hearing this and telling my pastor, "I am needed in the parish, and to be honest with you, I enjoy pastoral work. Besides this, I am now chaplain to the fire department, which I really like!" "Go back to school, Gino," he replied, "They can never take away your education!" He then added, "And I will pay for it!"

I followed his advice and began part-time courses at Loyola University in Chicago. Once into them, I realized the insufficiency of our seminary courses. The new ground-breaking ideas I received at the university completely changed the way I prepared and delivered homilies. I became much more aware of the sociological and psychological needs of the people in the pews. Thanks to courses in psychology—which we didn't have then in the seminary—I learned what to do and what to avoid when counseling people. Although I am grateful for my seminary education, returning to school after ordination was like a song we often hear at weddings, "We've Only Just Begun."

Through all of this, I also had a change of heart about study. Instead of seeing it as drudgery, I began to see it in terms of music. As great musicians always seek newness in a piece of classical music, I also was now seeking newness in ideas. Without sounding romantic, I now was seeking new melodies within old melodies that I had heard repeatedly. My mind was invigorated, giving me the exhilarating feeling of growing in new ideas and knowledge.

I further learned that taking a class with others has a delightful dimension that often isn't stressed: the principle of informal education. Stated simply, there are times we can learn more in informal conversations than we can from formal education. This held true especially at Loyola when other priests and I gathered for lunch or rode home together. Often the ideas discussed with them were as new and profound as those we received in the classroom.

No doubt many of us love our pastoral work and have little interest in leaving it, even if only for a day. This is understandable, especially for priests coming from second and third careers in which they were often going to seminars to update their professions. As true as this may be, it might do us well to ask, "Is total devotion to pastoral ministry the optimum model for today's priest, or is our present era calling for a new model that better balances the life of the mind with the life of our parish ministry?"

It is a fact that the present predicament of fewer priests and multiple responsibilities has locked us into parochial settings and walled us in. The word *kremlin* in Russian means "wall." One reason Russia became modernized during the reign of Peter the Great in the eighteenth century was his visits to other countries, where he learned how others built ships and managed commerce. Because of his ventures and the ideas he brought back to Russia, what had once been a status-quo country became progressive, outward looking, and a mighty world power. I believe the "Peter the Great Principle" suggests one good way for us to move beyond the walls of our parishes. Even though Peter the Great was the czar of an enormous country, he was able to travel, study, and learn because he knew how to delegate. There were times when those to whom he delegated power failed, forcing him to return home quickly. Yet for most of his life he was able to breach the walls of the Kremlin successfully. The art of delegation was one of the secrets behind Peter the Great's success. His innate passion for learning also drove him to move beyond the walls of the Kremlin. He exemplified the principle that "Passion for learning overcomes all barriers to it!"

Allow me to expand on this thought with a personal reflection from my pastoral ministry. I worked with a pastor of a large, busy parish who practiced the Peter the Great Principle par excellence. To his credit, he knew how to delegate. This allowed him to attend seminars and classes not only in the local area, but also nationally. When he returned, it was like taking a course in the latest ways of improving our ministry. The end result of his intellectual ventures was a parish that was anything but stagnant and status quo. Rather, it was filled with the life of the mind and was the envy of the diocese.

Let's look at some unique alternatives found in our own back yard for keeping our minds invigorated. One such alternative is the Internet. Once on it, enormous information is at our fingertips, requiring only a click to access it. All we need do is to be disposed to employing it. When we created the Web site of the National Institute for the Renewal of the Priesthood, we learned that not everyone is well disposed toward the Internet. Some of our priests still mistrust it. One bishop we interviewed on this subject objected that priests get on it and waste time, time that could be used more fruitfully for pastoral ministry. There is some justification for mistrusting the Internet, given some of the misinformation posted on it. And, it is a fact many of us waste enormous amounts of time surfing the net. However, if we plug the words "the Vatican" or "the United States Conference of Catholic Bishops" into a search engine, we learn that the Church has not only come to trust this new means of communication, but advocates it as a fruitful means for evangelization. We can sympathize with those who spurn the age of the Internet, but need not agree with them. To be true to our prophetic side, it is our responsibility to read the signs of the times and to employ the best means available for spreading the word of God. One such sign of the times is the Internet.

In addition to the Internet, we now have CDs, iPods™, kindle™, and BlackBerry® that can hold volumes of valuable information. The wonderful thing about them is that they can go anywhere we go. If we have more than one parish, what better way to utilize our travel time than listening to courses provided on a CD?

Another excellent means for upgrading our education is present in that daily companion of ours called the Breviary. When prayed well, it treats us to the best wisdom we could ever hope to obtain. All we need do is meditate on the readings and psalms intelligently and internalize them. This, however, is not as simple as it may sound.

Years ago, the philosopher and educator Mortimer Adler wrote a book entitled *How to Read a Book*. In it, Adler lists the basic rules of intelligent reading. When we read between the lines of these requirements, it becomes apparent that intelligent reading requires discipline and the formation of good habits. In the works of St. Ignatius of Loyola that focus on fruitfully meditating upon the scriptures, he moves us beyond Adler's principles by imploring us to enter into the minds and scenes of the scriptures and to practice *historia*: putting ourselves into the situation.

Whether we are following the discipline of Adler, St. Ignatius, or other spiritual writers when meditating on the scriptures, one fact remains: if we can truly enter into our breviary, then the knowledge, wisdom, and prudence we will learn far outweigh anything we could learn in the classroom.

I must confess it took me a very long time to befriend the Breviary. What captivated my interest in it grew out of the necessity of giving daily homilies, many of which were on feast days. In our breviary, we often have the original writings of the saint of the day. I began to study those writings carefully and found—to my delight—that they gave me all I needed for my homily. Not only that, but they took me much more deeply into the spiritualities of the saints; I never ceased to be surprised by how many refreshing spiritualities are revealed in their lives. I also learned that even though we often say the same psalms repeatedly, they always have something new to tell us. What moved me into this understanding was reading them in Spanish, which is a much more colorful and romantic language than English. Spanish brought the psalms to life.

Yet another practice for keeping our mental capacities invigorated is connecting with intelligent people. One fruitful conversation with a well-informed, educated person can equal many hours of classroom learning. I'll never forget the first time I realized this. One early morning while opening the church, a gentleman who had been waiting outside yelled at me, "You're late!" I retaliated by telling him that he was wrong and then ushered him into the sacristy to serve the Mass I celebrated. Weeks later we mended our fences and became the best of friends. Later I learned he was a doctor and worked as an associate researcher with a Nobel Prize winner who had discovered a life-threatening gene. One week while I was having difficulty writing a column on medical ethics, I stopped my friend after Mass and explained my dilemma. The conversation that followed was priceless. He opened up medical vistas I never would have seen. Within thirty minutes I not only had a course in the complexity of medical breakthroughs, I also had a first-class course in the medical-moral dilemmas that scientists face. This experience helped me realize that knowledge, ideas, and wisdom are in our own back yard; all we need do is humbly seek them.

When all is said and done, there is no justification whatsoever for letting our intellectual life slide. As true as this is, many of us often do let it slide to the point that we no longer have a real taste for serious study, research, and ongoing education. Even sadder is the fact that we aren't held accountable. There are a number of reasons for this. The first is that most of us—rightly so—regard pastoral ministry as the priority. Our ministry is seen in light of the spiritual and corporal works of mercy and the Church's sacramental life. This is where we desire to put most of our time and energy. Another reason why study, research, and ongoing education are not pursued in earnest is because they are not made compulsory; rather, they are considered a personal preference, voluntary.

At dinner one night, I was asked by friends, "What are you presently into?" I replied that I was writing this book, and at the moment was working on the chapter about ongoing education for priests. Our conversation then turned to the subject of ongoing education itself and how it is a requirement in most professions. I had to confess that with the exception of making a priest convocation or clergy day a requirement, the Church doesn't follow other professional organizations in making ongoing education mandatory, as is the case for my friends. Ongoing education was simply a requirement for them that often took the form of all-day seminars or periodic updates over the course of a year. As I listened to them, I thought of my sisters, one of whom is a physical therapist and the other in charge of a school district. They always tell me of learning about the latest developments in their respective fields.

Although many of us don't like to have the word "professional" applied to pastoral ministry, we are—in addition to being spiritual leaders—professionals in the sense that it is our responsibility to cultivate the life of the mind. We live in a time when the ongoing cultivation of the mind is imperative in order to avoid being ineffective. Unlike priests of the past, most of us have multiple parishes and our parishioners are seeking our spiritual guidance to help them through a much more complex life. Our best hope not only for coping with these challenges but taking them by the horns is to raise our cognitive powers to new levels, and to believe that study is ministry! There is no reason to let ourselves be backed into that dangerous corner of just "hanging on for dear life." We have numerous means at our disposal for going on the offensive. All we need is to be well disposed to study and just do it!

A man ought to handle his body like the sail of a ship, and neither lower and reduce it much when no cloud is in sight, nor be slack and careless in managing it when he comes to suspect something is wrong.

PLUTARCH (46–120), GREEK BIOGRAPHER AND PHILOSOPHER

WHAT IF WE WERE HEALTHIER?

WE KNOW THAT a well-rounded prayer life is one of the essentials of priestly life and ministry. It is essential, too, that priests continue their education, continue to learn. But when we talk about the essentials of priestly life, we definitely should not leave physical fitness out of the picture. "Health," the French essayist Michel de Montaigne counsels us, "is a precious thing, and the only one, in truth, which deserves that we employ in its pursuit not only time, sweat, trouble, and worldly goods, but even life . . . As far as I am concerned, no road that would lead us to health is either arduous or expensive."

What Montaigne said may be true, but does that justify placing health and physical fitness on a level with prayer and study? One very good reason for doing so is that prayer and study call for fitness. It is difficult to pray and study when we are tired and sluggish. The renowned football coach Vince Lombardi once said, "Fatigue makes cowards out of us!" When we aren't as healthy as we should be, more often than not we tend to take shortcuts in our ministry. The dividends of fitness are many: lower blood pressure, better eating habits, proper sleep, restorative relaxation, and just feeling good about oneself. Fitness tends to help us take the offensive—to attack challenges with vigor and not run from them.

I will never forget my first days at the U.S. bishops' conference in Washington, D.C., and the anxiety I experienced. One morning I was so nervous about my new responsibilities that I literally bounced off the walls as I ascended the steps to my office. I remember thinking I would end up in the hospital if I didn't find an antidote—a safety valve—for my anxiety. Within a few months I found that safety valve in running marathons. This, in turn, turned me into a devoted practitioner of exercise. What really hooked me on fitness were its benefits for my ministry. I found it easier to bring closure to tasks. It brought greater enthusiasm and zest to my work, and I had more patience.

Like most of us, I detest meetings and the patience of a Job that they require. Patience means not letting anything break our spirit. My new fitness routine not only made me healthier, but—more importantly—it strengthened my spirit against petty annoyances and the bizarre situations one often experiences. What would happen in our ministry if we were able to commit ourselves to just a little more physical fitness? One very real possibility is that we would practice better the kindness that people most want from their priests.

In a psychology class I attended, the professor often quoted Christ's admonition, "You shall love your neighbor as yourself" (Matthew 19:19). He urged us to take note that "self love comes first in order to love another." When applied to physical fitness, this commandment of Christ teaches us that the more we do something good for ourselves—like becoming more fit—the more we will like ourselves. In turn, the possibility increases that we will become kinder toward those we serve.

On our Web site, we post success stories that are especially aimed at helping priests stay physically, mentally, and spiritually fit. Below is one of those success stories related to fitness.

> A unique twelve-week fitness project for Baltimore City priests developed by Good Samaritan Hospital and sponsored by *The Catholic Review*, Baltimore's archdiocesan newspaper, is helping priests become fitter and significantly reduce their risk for heart disease. The experimental program allows archdiocesan priests, who rarely have time to exercise regularly, access to the hospital's Good Health Center any time of day or night.

> Father Richard Florek, OFM, 56, says, "If it hadn't been for that time flexibility, I don't think I could have kept up the five times a week I was able to do." This was seconded by other priests who said the program reduced feelings of stress and improved their attitude toward staying healthy as major benefits of the experience. And all of them want to continue the exercise program.

> Other priests from the archdiocese, like Father Joseph L. Muth, Jr., 52, reported that the program provided "a feeling of time-out" by helping him turn down his stress level and trim his waistline. Father James P. Farmer, 53, lost ten pounds and increased his strength and

flexibility. He also found the program "helped to improve my ability to relax." Father Richard J. Bozzelli, 40, "developed a new attitude toward health," becoming enlightened about how easily it can be obtained "with just a little effort." His overall risk for heart disease was reduced by 11 percent.

Father Patrick M. Carrion, 45, worked out with some regularity before entering the Good Samaritan program, but found it "challenged me to do even more. It raised the bar for me personally." Those priests who invested the most time reaped the most health rewards. Most encouraging of all was the participants' commitment to the program and the desire it provoked in them to increase or add to their lifestyles regular exercise and more thoughtful attention to their diets.[41]

All the priests who said they wanted to continue the program were no doubt motivated by its ability to reduce stress and weight. I believe it is also true that they were happier with themselves and, as a result, better disposed toward their people. The beauty of a success story like this is its ability to inspire us to duplicate it. Hospitals are always looking for ways to practice preventative medicine and keep people well. If there is a hospital near us, it might add years to our life and also make our ministry more fruitful if we investigate the possibility of partaking in a fitness program there. If this isn't possible, why not look around the area for a fitness club? The means at our disposal for staying fit are many. All we need do is to employ them.

I have known priests, and for that matter lay people, who cringe at the idea of physical exercise. They want no part of the kind of intensive exercises that bring one to the dropping point. In the article "The Softer Side of Fitness," the coordinator of fitness and physical therapy at Saint Luke Institute in Silver Springs, Maryland, Dana Dowd, describes another side of fitness that we seldom consider. "A client once explained to me that he did a triathlon (three-event work-out) every time he went to the gym: the sauna, the steam room, and the whirlpool. While he thought he was making a joke, I actually commended him on his efforts because he had made a commitment to do something that was good for his body, and he used a variety of treatments."[42] Dowd's comments teach us that physical fitness does not always have to be strenuous. What is important is the mind-set that physical well-being depends on doing "something" physically good for ourselves.

Dowd goes on to list other less strenuous but beneficial ways to stay in shape.

> On the other end of the continuum [of intense exercise] are relaxation exercises. These include anything that decreases our stress responses, e.g., lowers heart rate, breath rate, blood pressure, sweating and muscle activity, and increases temperature at the extremities. This phase includes meditation, feldenkrais, biofeedback training, massage, tai chi, certain aspects of Pilates and yoga, stretching, and breath training. These types of activities deactivate the body, promoting muscle relaxation, proper breathing patterns, and healing.[43]

During a walk on Capitol Hill early one morning, I came upon a priest I knew who was performing an Eastern exercise routine in a park near the Capitol. On first appearance, it didn't impress me as legitimate exercise. After all, I was running marathons, the ultimate in tough exercise. All he was performing were silent, still poses that involved little to no action. Later I learned this exercise routine was his way of starting the day relaxed and focused. It was also his means of fending off the depression that periodically plagued him. As I reflected on this, I realized that there are other beneficial means for staying fit besides excruciating marathons. He was a living example of Dowd's alternative of nonstrenuous exercise that produces true fitness.

During one of the yearly seminars convened by the J.S. Paluch Company in Chicago for vocation directors, I learned of yet another side of fitness that Dowd would approve: cultivating the art of beneficial rest. The presenter began by discussing the qualities a vocation director should possess. Suddenly he startled us when he seemed to go off on a tangent and began stressing the healing powers of rest. I thought to myself, "What does rest have to do with being a good vocation director?" As he continued, I began to see that rest, healing, fitness, and excellence in ministry are seldom, if ever, connected with each other. Usually excellence is connected with successful programs, but seldom with the fitness of the people behind the success. As devoted shepherds we often only see ourselves performing the unending task of caring for our sheep. Thinking of getting good sleep and cultivating rest seems so contrary to the messianic complex many of us have. Our American workaholic atmosphere also has much to do with leaving rest out of the picture. Working long, intensive hours to achieve a goal—even if it means collapsing under the pressure—is often lauded as heroic.

Embracing a hard-work philosophy is justifiable and to be desired, as long as we don't cross the line of prudence. Far too many priests have dropped out of active ministry, or even out of the priesthood, because they lost their ability to take proper rest. Many of them, sad to say, had a messianic complex in which they believed that everything began and ended with them. They didn't know how to delegate prudently. They didn't know how to say "no." They never came to realize that each and every phone call did not need to be returned immediately. Most of all, they didn't realize that ministry is accompanied by "injuries" and that healing them depended heavily on proper rest.

Hyperactive ministry that leads to a neglect of the rest we need also tends to dull our contemplative edge and our ability truly to celebrate life. It is so easy to become fidgety when we are out of shape and haven't had proper rest. This in turn weakens our powers of gazing and peering into our ministry to relish its beauty. The Roman politician and writer Pliny the Younger reminds us, "The body must be repaired and supported, if we would preserve the mind in all its vigor." We can add, "and especially to preserve the mind's ability to gaze, drink in the beauty of our ministry, and to celebrate it."

In the early years of St. Procopius Abbey in Lisle, Illinois, the abbey had a seminary run by the Benedictines. It was there I learned of an old, wise means for staying fit. One of the elderly monks periodically would tell his students, "You've got enough under your scull caps, now it's time to get dirt under your fingernails." And off the seminarians would march to work in the monastery garden or on the grounds. When I told this story to the abbot of St. Vincent's Benedictine Archabbey in Latrobe, Pennsylvania, he replied, "We have several elderly monks who have gardens. Yes, it is very Benedictine, and also extremely therapeutic!"

Up to this point, we have focused on the theme, *Mens sana, in corpore sano* or "Sound mind, sound body." Another theme we need to apply to fitness is, "Sound relationships, sound fitness!"

Studies have repeatedly shown that people who own pets or are consistently around animals tend to be healthier. One of my psychology professors once remarked that before automobiles came into existence, people had horses that needed tending. Caring for another, even a horse or farm animal, was very therapeutic and healthy because it forced people to get outside of themselves. Just as getting away from our work for a day can infuse us with new life, so getting outside oneself psychologically is a way of restoring fitness.

G. K. Chesterton had a unique take on this principle in his description of what he termed a "lunatic." A lunatic, he said, is a person who is like the moon. The moon is a circle with no outlets. A lunatic is a person who has inscribed himself or herself in a circle with no outlets. Today, we have a growing number of lone rangers in the priesthood who need to heed the advice of Chesterton and that old Benedictine. Serving multiple parishes and living alone can easily cause us to fall into unhealthy patterns. We may not become lunatics, but being alone has been known to spawn alcoholism, depression, and other troubling behaviors.

I have spent most of my priesthood living in community. Thanks to other priests and religious brothers with whom I lived, I had "mirrors" that enabled me to see myself from the outside. At one time I was chaplain to the Holy Cross Brothers at the University of Notre Dame. I will never forget the brothers telling me, "Father, with all due respect, you got that upside down in your homily this morning." They were mirrors that helped me see that I was veering away from the truth.

When I lived in the staff house of the bishops' conference, I had a stretch of ill health that I attributed to too much marathon training. One day a close friend said, "I don't think you are eating properly." I took his observation to heart and recovered immediately. He was a mirror who reflected to me the bad eating habits of which I had become unaware.

Companions not only serve as mirrors, but also help us to be more self-aware. Having a good companion is one of the biggest assets we can have for staying in shape, especially if the companion is frank. Those of us who live alone need to remember that fitness and good companionship are not only complementary, but absolutely necessary for a wholesome priesthood. I don't know how true it is today, but in the past, seminarians would joke about "jocks" and men who were "into" fitness. This was considered "body cult," and inappropriate. It didn't fit the picture of a true, hard-working, spiritual priest. In fact, if a priest looked too fit, it was common to hear others jokingly ask, "When do you work?" as if looking fit and working hard were antithetical to each other. Today, this no longer is a joking matter. Too many priests and bishops are on a leave of absence due to neglecting their fitness. Study and prayer are essential in ministry, and so are good health and fitness!

*The first step in the evolution of ethics is a
sense of solidarity with other human beings.*

ALBERT SCHWEITZER (1875–1965)

*[Make] every effort to maintain the unity of
the Spirit in the bond of peace.*

EPHESIANS 4:3

6

SOLIDARITY AT ITS BEST

HALF WAY THROUGH the clergy conference, I had the distinct impression that things were going awry. An unfriendly mood seemed to fill the air. During the evening happy hour, I asked one of the participants, "Is there something I said that is causing hostility?" "Gene, it's not you," he replied. "Our men are really angry because the bishop recently told us there is no priest shortage. Add to this the fact that we had planned a week-long meeting to discuss the shortage, and we were told we couldn't leave our parishes vacant. Hence the animosity you are sensing."

Is there a real priest shortage, and if so, is it critical, and what should be our priestly role in responding to it?

Some years ago, the head of Navy chaplains paid me a visit to show me the latest statistics on military Catholic chaplains. "Gene, look at these!" he exclaimed. "Our Catholic servicemen and servicewomen don't have enough Catholic chaplains to serve them!" He was correct then, and would be even more correct today. We don't have sufficient numbers of military chaplains to serve our armed forces around the world. In this particular arena, the shortage of priests is very real. Unfortunately, this not only holds true for military chaplains, but for a number of other Church ministries. The number of priests we need is simply greater than the number who are available. But there is more to the shortage of priests, however, than insufficient numbers.

Although the laity and permanent deacons are often the backbone of Church ministries, one of the most important ingredients in ministry is diminishing: our priestly presence. When we are absent, the assembly—the *ecclesia*—is incomplete. The priest shortage is so real that this incompleteness is accepted as the norm in many areas. Priests are becoming less integral to our faith communities! Priests who serve several parishes feel this acutely. To fully engage and participate in their parishes is almost impossible.

Priests becoming less of an integral part of their communities and communities without full-time priests are realities that point to a real shortage of priests. But can this shortage be deemed critical? Is the faith of our people suffering because of it? We are not talking about the community suffering from being incomplete. Rather, we are addressing its faith level: are we lacking the personnel needed to strengthen our Church? The answer is a resounding "no", according to all Church statistics. Three corps of people, when combined with our native-born priests, make up the personnel needed to keep the Church strong. Who are these corps, and what is our primary role in working with them?

We are talking about international priests, permanent deacons, and lay ministers. A bird's-eye view of them reveals the reality that we are very blessed with dedicated ministers serving the Church.

The 2007 study *International Priests in America*[44] estimates that we have approximately 5,500 international priests in the United States. Thirteen percent are religious priests, and 87 percent are diocesan priests. It is estimated that between 380 and 400 international priests enter this country each year. These priests are usually much younger than native-born priests. If, as is presently happening, their average age continues to remain relatively low and they continue to immigrate to and remain in the United States, the priesthood may soon take on a new look in terms of cultural diversity. One very good reason for asserting this is that many professions in our country are experiencing an influx of professionals from other countries.

Other statistics of interest reveal that 28 percent of seminarians training for the priesthood are international students. One-third of the diocesan and religious international priests expect to stay in the United States more than five years, and a little more than 40 percent are uncertain whether they will stay or go home to their native lands.

Four major arguments are lodged against recruiting international priests for the United States:

1. There are too many potential challenges with them— mainly in language and culture.

2. Bringing priests to the United States is an irrational deployment of priestly resources in the world.

3. Bringing priests to the United States postpones a much-needed restructuring of parish leadership.

4. Bringing priests to the United States thwarts lay efforts to recruit more vocations in our country.

In the interviews I conducted for the study on international priests, one parish minister told me, "As much as we Americans are familiar with our culture, connecting with our youth culture is extremely difficult. An international priest who is unfamiliar with the culture and who ministers to our youth, more often than not, compounds the problem of reaching our teens." Whenever the question of international priests is raised, so too, are the perceived problems they present. In a number of cases, they feel unwelcome because they are deemed more problematic than helpful.

It is a fact that international priests will continue to migrate to this country in larger numbers and add substantially to our ranks due to our new age of globalization. It is also a fact that many of our international priests enrich our culture and the Church in the United States. What is most important now is to open our hearts and minds to them. In one of the interviews I conducted concerning this issue, I learned of a diocesan program that did exactly this. The diocese not only threw open its arms to international priests but walked arm and arm with them. Lay mentor teams were created to assist them in knowing where best to shop, find a good doctor, get an automobile license, and to help them understand cultural differences. Not only this, to show their gratitude, the diocese sent volunteers to the country from which these international priests came. *International Priests in America* documents similar stories that demonstrate that "where there is a will, there is a way; where there is vision good things happen!" I believe the ratio of successes to failures generated by the influx of international priests reveals that they generate more success stories than problems.

I will never forget serving at Mass for a priest from India when I was a young man. Every word he spoke was clothed in respect, and his gestures were ever so sacred. He left a beautiful impression on me, which, to this day, inspires me to imitate his manner of celebrating Mass.

There were many times when I celebrated Mass with Latino priests and experienced a ritual vitality that filled the liturgy with joy, reflecting the joy of being with God. I have also had a similar experience when celebrating Mass with African American priests. I will never forget my early childhood in which Irish-born priests greeted us with their beautiful brogues and their uplifting spirits.

There is no doubt that many of us have been inspired by the manner in which people from other cultures not only celebrate the sacraments, but leave a lasting and wholesome impression on us. They are embodiments of the work of the Holy Spirit as they enrich us with the new life and inspiration that multiculturalism possesses.

A researcher once remarked, "It doesn't take long to become enculturated when dioceses have well-thought-out programs and comprehensive policies for international priests. As many of our grandparents integrated into this country and became its backbone, so too can our international priests with the right organizational procedures and policies." We might add that more important than well-thought out programs and policies is attitude! We are one universal priesthood, no matter our country and culture. We are not *us and them*, but *we*! To the degree that we embrace our oneness, our Church will benefit from the new American priesthood that is growing in our country.

The second corps of persons who strengthen our Church is permanent deacons. The number of deacons in the United States continues to increase. They now total an estimated 16,661, of whom 78 percent are in active ministry. Ninety-three percent of active deacons are married and 4 percent are widowed. Twenty-five percent are age seventy or older, 36 percent are in their sixties, 29 percent are in their fifties, 10 percent are in their forties, and 1 percent are age thirty-nine or younger.

By race/ethnicity, 81 percent of active deacons are non-Hispanic white, 15 percent are Hispanic/Latino, 2 percent African American/black, 1 percent are Asian, and 1 percent are Native American or some other race or ethnicity. More than half of the active deacons have at least a bachelor's degree and 19 percent have a master's degree. About four in ten active deacons are paid for their ministry in a parish (11 percent full-time and 30 percent part-time). More than a third of deacons work full- or part-time in secular occupations.[45]

In the two national studies we conducted on deacons, one in 1981 and the second in 1995, five major issues were noted.

1. The diaconate needs to recruit younger men in order to be vibrant and better balanced.

2. Between the 1981 study and the 1995 study, the average age of deacons increased from 50 to 60 years old.

3. A substantial number of deacons tend to hover around the sacristy more and minister in the marketplace less. A complaint lodged against some deacons is that they are nothing more than "glorified altar boys." (It should be noted that many of our deacons are retired and no longer work in the marketplace, hence, one reason they are less involved in the marketplace. It should also be noted that there has been very little written on what role in particular a deacon is expected to fulfill in the marketplace.)

4. Deacons are sometimes taken advantage of, and the more difficult and challenging facets of ministry often end up in their laps.

5. Deacons in general, and those who minister in hospitals especially, should be able to administer the sacrament of the anointing of the sick.

Given the need to work through these issues better, most priests who have deacons agree they are an added blessing for keeping our faith alive. In general, they personify the corporal and spiritual works of mercy par excellence.

One dimension of the diaconate that is often overlooked is the fact that the majority of deacons are married. When we envision the diaconate, their wives need to be seen as part of the equation. In addition to lending moral support, many wives are co-workers in their husband's ministry and their ministry needs to be acknowledged, supported, and encouraged.

The third corps essential to our ministry is the growing number of lay ministers. Of the 308 active lay ecclesial ministry formation programs identified in 2006–07, the Center for Applied Research in the Apostolate (CARA) reported that 253 or 82 percent responded to their survey.[46] This high return gives us a very reliable picture of lay ministry. These programs report a total of 20,240 lay ecclesial ministry candidates, of whom 13,523 (67 percent) are working toward a certificate in ministry and 6,717 (33 percent) are seeking a graduate degree in ministry. This represents a 26 percent increase over the total reported by 226 programs in 2005–06.

Distance learning and online course work are growing aspects of lay ministry formation. Directors of formation programs responded as follows to the question, "Is any part of your program offered online?" Thirty-two percent said students can enroll online, 22 percent offer course work online, and 1 percent offers degree completion online.

Academic formation and certification are central to lay ministry formation, but spiritual formation and practical experience are also important components of preparation for ministry. Of the 253 active programs, 55 percent say that formal spiritual development is required, and 48 percent say the program includes a field education/internship requirement. Some programs (37 percent) require both.

The profile of lay ecclesial ministry formation program participants finds that 64 percent are lay women, 33 percent lay men, 2 percent women religious, and 1 percent religious brothers. Six in ten students are in their forties and fifties, with 27 percent under age forty and 13 percent age sixty or older. Seventy-one percent are white, 18 percent Hispanic/Latino, 4 percent are black, 3 percent are Asian, and 4 percent are of another culture.

Lay ministers have always outnumbered ordained clergy. They are, and always have been, the right arm of the Church and the most potent force for keeping the Church's faith strong. This is especially true of lay women ministers, who make up approximately two-thirds of all lay ministers.

It is important to mention here that religious sisters and religious brothers come under the category of laity. When we study the unique roles they fulfill in the Church, we learn that it was they who kept our priesthood and Church afloat when the priest shortage first became critical. In numerous cases, religious sisters literally ran—and still run—parishes without a full-time pastor. This holds equally true of religious brothers who not only serve in parishes but also in other capacities that once were the responsibility of a priest. Allow me to cite two examples of the roles religious fulfill.

When I studied at the University of Notre Dame, as previously mentioned, I had the privilege of being the chaplain to the Holy Cross brothers. During my tenure, these brothers established a junior college. Since its establishment, it has helped thousands of students obtain degrees and go on to prestigious colleges and universities, students who otherwise never would have had this opportunity. This success was due in great part to the foresight and hard work of the Holy Cross brothers.

What was equally inspiring was experiencing the brothers who worked behind the scenes and supported their brother brothers who were staffing the college: cooks who provided excellent community meals, brothers who took care of the grounds and community automobiles, and those who maintained the buildings. This was the backup team behind the scenes of the junior college that ultimately helped thousands of young men and women get an education. This is just one of many success stories that must be told when speaking of keeping our Catholic faith alive.

These same success stories abound among our religious sisters. Some of the most memorable and substantive burial services I have ever experienced were by sisters who helped run parishes without a full-time pastor. And, too, a walk through many of our Catholic hospitals reveals dedicated sisters who are forever caring for the sick and in so doing reflect Christ our healer.

When the priest shortage is discussed, it is common to point to the statistics that show we have one priest for several thousand Catholics. This is a valid comparison. However, when the priesthood is combined with the above corps of ministers, the picture changes dramatically. In terms of personnel, credentials, and spirituality, the institutional Church is blessed with a strong corps of persons who are keeping the faith alive.

This brings us to our second question: what is the role of the priesthood in working with our co-workers in the vineyard? What should be our expectations?

I believe the times are calling for the cultivation of a new type of solidarity that takes the idea of *communio* deeper. A concern and focus of the Bishops' Subcommittee on Lay

Ministry asserts, "Lay ecclesial ministry and the ministry of the ordained complement each other within the dynamic *communio* of the Church. They are not in competition . . . The ordained and the laity share in one ministry of Christ and, in their distinctive roles, work toward accomplishing the one mission that Christ has given the Church."[47]

The solidarity of which we speak pictures us not only working together harmoniously in our respective roles, but working as a more tightly knit team. This is in opposition to thinking and acting in terms of bailiwicks, domains, groupings, turfs, juridical boundaries, and yes, even in terms of our own personal unique gifts and individuality. It is solidarity based on the spiritual principle of self-abandonment for the good of others, and especially the work of God. An episode from history exemplifies this solidarity.

A century after Julius Caesar invaded Britain, the emperor Claudius launched a major expedition—in AD 43—and imposed Roman rule in southern England. The Britons despised Roman domination and its taxes. In AD 60, Boudicca, queen of the British tribe Iceni, led a major insurrection against the Roman colonies and slaughtered seventy thousand Romans. In response to this onslaught, Rome assigned Gnaeus Julius Agricola, a Roman statesman and general, to put down the revolt.

Following skirmishes, the Roman legions and Boudicca's tribes found themselves facing off on a hillside surrounded by forests. The hordes of Iceni that Boudicca mustered far outnumbered the Roman legions, and by all odds should have overwhelmed and slaughtered them.

As the battle began, Roman javelin throwers and archers sent oceans of spears and arrows into Boudicca's advancing army. Then the Roman legion marched their phalanxes into the fray. A phalanx consisted of highly trained Roman soldiers armed with swords, spears, and shields. Several rows of men marching shoulder to shoulder in columns formed square boxes. Those on the outside of the column and those in its middle locked shields, forming protective walls against oncoming ballistics. The role of the soldiers in the front line was to hack away with their swords and stab with their spears anything in front of them. When they became tired, they rotated back and the next line came forward. The phalanxes moved in on Boudicca's forces, splitting them and making them less effective. The end result was total defeat.

Although the idea of a phalanx dates back to ancient history, it has much to teach us about the need of a more vigorous solidarity today. It first teaches that a phalanx depends on well-trained, elite soldiers. Second, successfully winning a battle depends on men who care for, fight for, and if necessary, die for each other. Lastly, it consists of a team spirit of working together shoulder to shoulder.

These days, it goes without saying that anyone who is truly devoted to his or her ministry is in for a battle that often threatens to overwhelm him or her. On our home front, we have, among other things, the issues of reaching our youth, integrating and living side by side with a new wave of cultures, and finding fresh methods for reaching those who have left the Church. We have the poor, the depressed, those fighting chemical dependency, and those in hospice care. There are families desperately searching for ways to remain together. We see growing addiction to Internet pornography. These are just the tip of the iceberg of weighty challenges in our back yard.

On a more global front, we are being challenged to respond to medical and scientific moral questions, ecological concerns, the need for stewardship of the earth's resources, the question of war and genocide, the spread of deadly diseases, and the needs of our destitute brothers and sisters around the world. The list of issues needing our attention and ministry is endless. How to remain focused is often difficult, if not impossible.

The issues we priests need to face are numerous: how to generate solidarity, how to become knit together more closely with our people, how to create greater effectiveness and efficiency, and especially how to maintain an undaunted spirit.

In a Roman legion, each soldier was tattooed, signifying that he was part of an elite corps. Interestingly, the *sphragis*, which is the sign of the cross we make over a newly baptized child, receives one of its meanings from the Roman tattoo, symbolizing becoming an elite member of a community. As Roman soldiers received a mark denoting their specialness, so too are our three corps of ministers specially marked. In devoting themselves to Church ministry and being acclaimed by the community as special ecclesial ministers, they are an elite corps in the sense of being specially schooled and at the service of God and the community. Like the Romans, we have created ceremonies to symbolize the uniqueness of their callings. But once the ceremonies are over, what further needs to be done to draw out the concrete actions connoted by these symbols?

In retreats I conduct, there is a session in which five or more priests tell the story of their journey through the priesthood. It is by far the most powerful session of the retreat. It also gives us a good model of how to generate stronger solidarity. These sessions are powerful for a number of reasons. Almost always we learn of particular hidden charisms with which priests are blessed, charisms of which often their closest friends had no awareness. Suddenly, there is a new realization that they are truly a blessing to the diocese, their people, and us.

In these sessions priests open up their hearts. After the session is over, it never fails that most priests linger and begin to share their journeys. It is no exaggeration to say that those moments are filled with a new sense of camaraderie and of solidarity. There is a heightened realization that everyone feels part of a special team of men who mutually share the same aspirations, problems, fears, and hopes. When we connect with each other on this level, when openness and sharing are more prevalent, when there is a feeling that we all share the same concerns, and when we more fully realize we have a unique—and yes—special calling, we are on our way to creating a close-knit corps and solidarity at its best. In order to sustain this connection, however, it must be backed up with a special spirit. And what might that spirit be?

In a study on marriage, it was asked what one thing above all others most helped marriages succeed? The answer was *interest*. Interest is at the heart of people communicating with each other. It keeps relationships fresh and, most of all, when we are interested in another it brings the best out of him or her. Sincere interest in another also causes us to watch out for the other. It is altruism par excellence!

This type of interest isn't about getting deeply involved in the personal lives of others, or becoming maternalistic or paternalistic. Rather, it is about a spirit in which we take time to learn of each other's talents, and the journeys we experienced in becoming co-workers in the vineyard.

When I was writing this book, people would ask what it was about. When I began to tell them, it never failed that their interest would wane, or they would take off on what I said and tell me what they have done in this area. This is all good and well, and is common in conversation. But it also reveals that when we say we are interested in another, sometimes this is more like the throw-away salutation "How are you?" than true interest. There is no focus, no listening, no true entering into, no real connection, and no solidarity.

Not only does interest encourage us to listen to and connect with others more fully, it also encourages us to leave our comfort zone and to enter the zones of others. When Pope Paul VI was a cardinal archbishop of Milan, he often disappeared from his office and couldn't be found. The reason no one knew where to find him was that he went to places they never thought a cardinal would visit on a regular basis: he went to the factories. He loved to converse with the workers about their work, their family life, and the challenging issues they faced. He was so interested in his people that he would often leave the confines of his comfortable palatial office to be with them.

Cardinal Claudio Hummes, the prefect of the Congregation for Clergy, once said, "When priests move, the Church moves." To move, however, means to have interest in others to the point that it moves us to be more intimately connected with them.

Interest takes us beyond *communio* in that it desires a spirit-to-spirit union. Perhaps this type of interest is too much to ask of us with our busy schedules. And yet, when we listen to persons like Cardinal John Henry Newman, Pope Benedict XVI, Cardinal Suhard, and Jim Lehrer, we immediately sense that our main interest as a priest should be "for" the other—supporting the other as if he or she is on the front line of a battle, standing shoulder to shoulder with those with whom we serve and have kindred interests.

During three decades of conducting Church studies, we have learned that a number of worthwhile improvements have been made in bringing priests, deacons, and the laity closer together. However, during those decades we also learned that we have repeatedly returned to our juridical differences and focused on how one ministry is not like another. As long as we have two people gathered together, the issues of drawing lines between roles will always exist. This is part of any institution. This is good as long as it doesn't become our main concern. If it does, it is an indication that the solidarity we should be practicing is lacking the spirit of true interest in each other that is needed to succeed.

When Cardinal Joseph Ratzinger, now Pope Benedict XVI, was elected, Church observers dug up every thing they could find about him. One thing they surfaced was his deep respect for the Eastern churches and their emphasis on spirit, which contrasts with the Roman Church's emphasis on the juridical. Laws are necessary for the good of an institution. But more often than not, it is spirit that gives an institution heart and vitality. Once the laws are stated, spirit must reign—a spirit of mutual interest in each other. What we as priests are being prompted to achieve when we speak of solidarity is to see ourselves as the catalyst of this spirit. As leader of the community, it is our responsibility to take the lead in generating solidarity and kindred interest through our words, and especially our example. This does not imply that we become an ombudsman, *the* teacher, *the* boss, *the* shepherd. Rather, it suggests a kind priestly heart earnestly endeavoring to bring hearts together as one. It is a disposition that says, "Each of us possesses a special calling, a unique mission that requires that we work together shoulder to shoulder. We need to be looking over our shoulder periodically for ways to support each other. We have a special responsibility to respond to each other as teammates, and to work together as a phalanx."

The objection may be raised that, although we do take deep interest in each other and try to create a team spirit, the reality is that we can't do all that is needed to make this happen fully. Because we are too rushed, too busy, too spread out, too undermanned, too tired, and sometimes too discouraged by all our responsibilities, the model of the phalanx, though inspiring, seems unrealistic for everyday ministry. We might be tempted to say that there is simply not enough energy to go around to make it happen. Is it really unrealistic if we are practicing will-to-meaning and the life this generates in us? Is it impossible if we are trying to practice kindness and working hard to create a positive disposition that is always looking for the optimum in our ministry? Is it improbable if we are supported with the resilience that contemplation generates, the vitality ongoing education begets, and the physical and mental strength that comes with fitness?

If the habits of the heart described in this book are taken seriously and we endeavor to do our best to practice them, the answer is a resounding one: "No, it is not unrealistic! We can and must do it!"

NOTES

[1] www.jknirp.com

[2] Robert N. Bellah, Richard Madsen, William M. Sullivan, Ann Swidler, and Steven Tipton, *Habits of the Heart* (Berkeley, CA: University of California Press, 1985), vii.

[3] Laurence J. Peter and Raymond Hull, *The Peter Principle.* Copyright © 1969 by William Morrow & Company, Inc. Reprinted by permission of HarperCollins Publishers. Published in the United Kingdom and British Commonwealth by Souvenir Press, London.

[4] Melvin Blanchette, James Castelli, Eugene Hemrick, Paul Theroux, James Walsh, *Grace Under Pressure: What Gives Life to American Priests: A Study of Effective Priests Ordained Ten to Thirty Years* (Washington, D.C.: National Catholic Educational Association, 1996), 12.

[5] Ibid., 19.

[6] Ibid., 45.

[7] Ibid., 52.

[8] Emmanuel Suhard, *The Collected Writings of Emmanuel Cardinal Suhard* (Chicago: Fides Publications, 1953), 273.

[9] Ibid.

[10] Dean Hoge, *Experiences of Priests Ordained Five to Nine Years: A Study of Recently Ordained Catholic Priests* (Washington, D.C.: National Catholic Educational Association, 2006), 50.

[11] Bernard Häring, CSSR, *The Church: Sacrament of Christ* (Liguori, MO: Liguori Celebrations Series, 1999), 39–40. © 1999, Munich Province of the Redemptorists. All rights reserved.

[12] *Catechism of the Catholic Church* No. 1547. Excerpts from the English translation of the Catechism of the Catholic Church for use in the United States of America Copyright © 1994, United States Catholic Conference, Inc.—*Libreria Editrice Vaticana*. Used with Permission. Internal quote from *Lumen Gentium* 10§2. Excerpts from *Vatican Council II, Volume I: The Conciliar and Post Conciliar Documents*, edited by Rev. Austin Flannery, O.P., copyright © 2007, Costello Publishing Company, Inc., Northport, NY, used by permission of the publisher, all rights reserved. No part of these excerpts may be reproduced, stored in a retrieval system, or transmitted in any form or by any means—electronic, mechanical, photocopying, recording or otherwise, without express permission of Costello Publishing Company, Inc.

[13] Romano Guardini, *The Virtues: On Forms of Moral Life* (Chicago: Henry Regnery Company, 1963), 82.

[14] Robert Waldron, *Thomas Merton: Master of Attention* (New York: Paulist Press, 2008), 52.

[15] Carlo Maria Martini, *In the Thick of His Ministry* (Middlegreen, England: St. Paul Publications, 1990), 13.

[16] Kieran Kavanaugh, *St. Teresa of Ávila for Every Day: Reflections from the Interior Castle* (New York: Paulist Press, 2006), 54.

[17] Evelyn Waugh, *Decline and Fall*, (New York: Little, Brown and Company).

[18] Merle Shain, *Hearts That We Broke Long Ago* (New York: Bantam Books, 1983), 35.

[19] Ted Keating, SM, "Improving Pastoral Care and Accountability in Response to the Tragedy of Sexual Abuse," Conference of Major Superiors of Men Annual Assembly. Philadelphia, PA. August 10, 2002.

[20] John Henry Newman, *The Idea of a University* (New Haven, CT: Yale University Press, 1996), 208–09.

[21] Excerpt from May 25, 2006 homily of Pope Benedict XVI © 2006, *Libreria Editrice Vaticana*. All rights reserved. Used with permission.

[22] Joseph Ratzinger, *Introduction to Christianity* (San Francisco: St. Ignatius Press, 2004), 189.

[23] Excerpt from speech given at the dedication of the National Museum of the Marine Corps in Quantico, Virginia on November 10, 2006. Copyright © 2006, Jim Lehrer. Used with permission.

[24] Anson Shupe, *Spoils of the Kingdom: Clergy Misconduct and Religious Community*. (Champaign, IL: University of Illinois Press, 2007), 56–57.

[25] Ibid.

[26] George B. Wilson, SJ, *Clericalism: The Death of Priesthood*, 16–31, 59, 122, 129, 130. Copyright © 2008 by the Order of Saint Benedict, Inc. Reprinted with permission of Liturgical Press Collegeville, MN 56321.

[27] From *Gift from the Sea* by Anne Morrow Lindbergh, copyright © 1955, 1975, renewed 1983 by Anne Morrow Lindbergh. Used by permission of Pantheon Books, a division of Random House, Inc.

[28] Romano Guardini, *Power and Responsibility: A Course of Action for the New Age* (Chicago: Henry Regnery Company, 1951), 99.

[29] Ibid.

[30] Rabbi Arthur Hertzberg, "The Long View from St. Meinrad," *National Catholic Reporter*, September 20, 1967, 10.

[31] Excerpt from Paragraph 4 of Pope Paul VI's *Apostolic Exhortation on Evangelization in the Modern World.* Copyright © 1975, *Liberia Editrice Vaticana.* All rights reserved. Used with permission.

[32] Theodore Cardinal McCarrick's Column, "My Catholic Standard," Washington, D.C. April 7, 2005. Copyright © 2005, *The Catholic Standard.* Used with permission.

[33] Romano Guardini, *Preparing Yourself for Mass* (Manchester, NH: Sophia Institute Press, 1997), 11.

[34] www.jknirp.com

[35] Walter J. Burghardt, "Priestly Preparation and Academic Excellence," NCEA, *Seminaries in Dialogue,* No. 16, September 1987, 1.

[36] John Henry Newman, *The Idea of a University,* (New Haven, CT: Yale University Press, 1996), 208–09.

[37] Michael Downey, ed., *The New Dictionary of Catholic Spirituality,* 783. Copyright © 1993 by the Order of Saint Benedict, Inc. Reprinted with permission of Liturgical Press Collegeville, MN 56321.

[38] Carole Ganim, *Shaping Catholic Parishes: Pastoral Leaders in the 21st Century* (Chicago: Loyola Press, 2008), 123–24.

[39] Excerpt from Paragraph 19 of Pope Paul VI's *Apostolic Exhortation on Evangelization in the Modern World.* Copyright © 1975, *Liberia Editrice Vaticana.* All rights reserved. Used with permission.

[40] Center for Applied Research in the Apostolate: The CARA Report: Vol. 13, No. 4, Spring 08, Georgetown University, Washington, D.C.

41 *The Catholic Review*, Baltimore, MD, July 2001.

42 Dana Dowd, M.S. P. T., "The Softer Side of Fitness," *Lukenotes*, Vol. X, No. 3 May/June 2006. *Lukenotes* is a publication of St. Luke Institute, Silver Spring, MD and is available online at www.sli.org.

43 Ibid.

44 Dean R. Hoge and Aniedi Okure, *International Priests in America*, 11-12. Copyright © 2006 by the Order of Saint Benedict, Inc. Reprinted with permission of Liturgical Press Collegeville, MN 56321.

45 Office of Research and the Bishops' Committee on the Permanent Diaconate, *A National Study on the Permanent Diaconate of the Catholic Church in the United States: 1994–1995* (Washington, D.C.: Publications Office of the United States Catholic Conference, 1996).

46 Center for Applied Research in the Apostolate: The CARA Report. Georgetown University, Washington, D.C.

47 Excerpt from *Lay Ecclesial Ministry: The State of the Questions*, Section: Toward a Theology of Lay Ecclesial Ministry, Part D, Conclusions 13 and 15. Copyright © 1999, United States Conference of Catholic Bishops, Inc., Washington, D.C. All rights reserved. Used with permission.

As Director of Research for the United States Conference of Catholic Bishops, Fr. Eugene Hemrick, a priest of the diocese of Joliet, Illinois, compiled extensive research on priests in the United States. He holds master's degrees in theology and religious education from St. Mary of the Lake Seminary and Loyola University Chicago. He also holds a Ph.D. in education from the University of Notre Dame. Currently, Fr. Hemrick writes a weekly syndicated national column for the

Catholic News Service. He is also the director of the National Institute for the Renewal of the Priesthood, an organization that provides a forum for priests to assist them in finding and maintaining the energy needed to serve the Catholics of this country and abroad. Fr. Hemrick has authored a number of books, including *The Promise of Virtue* (Ave Maria Press, 1999) and *Grace Under Pressure: What Gives Life to American Priests* (National Catholic Educational Association, 1995). Among the many awards and recognitions he has received is the Touchstone Award, conferred in April of 2009 by the National Federation of Priests' Councils. Fr. Hemrick resides in Washington, D.C., and serves as Director of Research at Washington Theological Union as well as parish priest for St. Joseph on Capitol Hill.